Learn to Sew in Minutes

Machine Sewing

DISCARD

First published in 2020

Search Press Limited
Wellwood, North Farm Road,
Tunbridge Wells, Kent TN2 3DR

SUPPLIERS

If you have any difficulty obtaining any of the
materials and equipment mentioned in this book,
please visit the Search Press website:
www.searchpress.com

Learn to Sew in **30** Minutes

Machine Sewing

25 quick & easy projects
to build your skills

Debbie von Grabler-Crozier

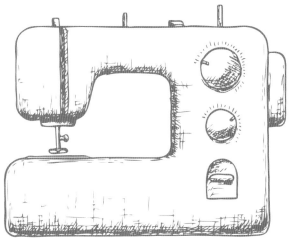

SEARCH PRESS

CONTENTS

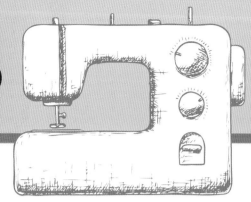

INTRODUCTION

I love a practical book; one that explains – AND shows you – how to do something, and then gives you the chance to make something yourself, using the same technique. Well, now we can check that box!

This book is designed as a practical course, teaching you how to machine sew through making a variety of projects. This means that right away, from the first lesson, you will put your new-found skills into practice and have something cute and useful to make and own.

I learnt to sew last century (I know, right) and I had my dedicated Nana and Mum to help me. There wasn't much to do in the middle of Australia in the 1970s, but there was a sewing machine and I loved it! My Nana had made all of her children's clothes and things for her home on that machine, and it was also the one on which she and my Mum taught me to sew. I still have that same machine now, to remember happy times.

But you know what? Even an experienced sewist like myself has a surprising number of limitations: recently, I was in my local haberdashery and I had to ask the lady about machine needles! You see, my Nana's antique Singer treadle machine had only one sewing foot and one needle. This meant I learnt to sew everything – zips, leather and all – with a single type of needle and foot, which meant I had to work around the limitations. I'd been doing the same thing for years on my new machines, and it came as a bit of a shock that I didn't need to – and shouldn't!

This taught me a lesson though: you are never too expert to stop learning! This book is all about that, and much more. Sewing is fun, learning is fun, and if you can do both you're heading straight for the win.

I was fortunate to learn how to machine sew the traditional way, from my mother and grandmother, but the new traditional way is with a book – something you can grab and journey through at your own pace. If you are a newbie, I hope you will find your feet with this book through these 30-minute lessons, each one supported by a fun project to put your new-found expertise into practice. If you have been sewing for a while you can still take something away – perhaps a new technique or ideas for quick gifts.

Have fun as you go on with your own journey; I will be with you every step of the way.

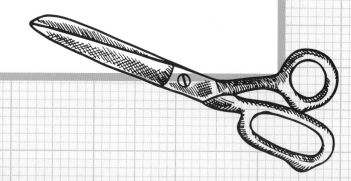

YOUR SEWING BOX

You actually don't need an awful lot to get started and make something useful (and amazing-looking too). The great thing about sewing, too, is that your stash will grow as you sew. Before long, you will have one of those enviable stash piles that we see all over social media. The chapters and projects in this book are designed to start you off with pretty much nothing and then show you how and when to build on what you have.

However, you and I know that you need a little bit of kit to get you going, so here are some of the things I cannot do without. Always buy the best that you can and have a look around in sales online or in store. This is a list more than anything else, and I will address each item as we meet it in the following chapters.

QUILTING COTTON

JERSEY

CANVAS

LINEN

FELT

LEATHER

INTERFACING

FABRICS

The scope of this book is to teach you how to sew homewares with a few different types of fabric. You will be pleased to know that we stay mainly with cotton, linen and felt, although feel free to interchange these in the patterns if you wish. A word of advice: these are nice, easy fabrics to machine sew, and I recommend sticking with them if you are a complete newbie. Once you're more confident with your machine-sewing skills, you can tackle fabrics that require unusual needles (such as knit fabrics like jersey) or slippery fabrics that are likely to shift (such as silk and crepe) – as these are in the realms of advanced sewing, these fabrics and their corresponding techniques and needles are not covered in this book. I will also look at some other, alternative fabrics when it comes to upcycling ideas, but they will be tackled as they come along. For more detailed information on cotton, linen, canvas, felt and leather, refer to Chapter 1 (pages 20–39).

If you want to start building a stash of fabrics (and who doesn't?), start looking for **fat quarters**. This is actually a quilting term, and you often see quilters abbreviate it to 'FQs'. These are technically a quartered yard of fabric, but instead of a quarter-yard strip (25cm/10in in new money) these fat-quarter cuts are a half-yard square of fabric – simply, a yard of fabric cut into quarters. Every quilting and fabric shop has these, almost always in cotton (known as **quilting cotton**), and there are some brilliant buys to be found in the sales. To show you how useful these cuts are, the first ten makes in this book use fat quarters!

Next is the **fat eighth** (or F8th). In the simplest of terms, a fat eighth is half of a fat quarter (as you would expect). However, it can be cut in two different ways. Cut style number one is cut vertically and is slightly chunkier; cut style number two is cut horizontally and is longer and thinner. It depends on what you want to use it for, of course. I prefer the chunkier cut because it is deeper, which I find more useful.

Some projects will use a couple more expensive – but not larger – cuts of fabric. **Felt** is one of these. You can buy felt in squares or by the metre. In the early stages look for squares because, like FQs, these are enough to get you started and will mean that you can afford a whole paint box of colours. I would pick wool-blend over acrylic felt for the same reason that I would avoid nylon and polyester when buying fabric. Acrylic felt doesn't look as nice, the colours are slightly too bright (and not in a nice way) and they never wear as well. I find also that acrylic felt stretches and distorts in an unpredictable way too. Not good. Go for natural every time.

Another, slightly more luxurious fabric is **leather**. For these, keep an eye out online for leather scrap bags – this is how I buy mine. They are cheaper to buy this way, as they are usually remnants from the textile industry (once, a particular bag came from an Italian jacket factory!), and this makes them suitable to sew with too. Buying bulk scraps of leather means I never know what colour or type I will get, but this is part of the fun! I adore these surprise packs, and I will show you as we go along how to make gorgeous embellishments with these, to really lift your items from 'homemade' to 'handmade'.

INTERFACING

This is a new thing for most sewing rookies. It is not seen once the project is finished, therefore many wonder if they can get away without it. Stop. Right. There.

Interfacing is what makes your fabric look good. It is underwear for your sewing project: like a good bra, it can lift an outfit. It is the foundation of your make and it should never be left out. I have actually seen some beautiful sewing let down because the maker left out interfacing. So, start building a stash of interfacing at the same time you buy fabric.

Always buy what the pattern advises, and try to learn to use different kinds to build your experience. Interfacing mainly comes in two types: woven and non-woven. Woven ones are pretty easy to spot because, like fabric, they have threads going up and threads going across to make a piece of fabric (there's a little more info about this on page 16). These can be whisper light or a little heavier. Non-woven interfacing looks very similar to felt.

Within these categories you then have fusible and sew-in interfacing. **Fusible** means that a glue has been applied to one side when it was made in the factory, and is designed to be stuck onto the wrong side of the fabric with an iron. You can easily feel which side is fusible and which is not, because the glue side will be either bumpier or shinier than the other side – for this reason, ALWAYS double check your interfacing before merrily ironing it on, making sure that the glue side is facing the back (or 'wrong side') of the fabric! If it is not, you will ruin your ironing board cover by fusing the interfacing to that. **Sew-in interfacing** is exactly what it says on the can. You cannot fuse it onto fabric because there is no glue. To apply it, you will need to lay your fabric panel on top and then sew it in place with a narrower-than-usual seam around the outside. (Don't panic if this makes no sense yet; it will!) I like to use non-preshrunk fabric for sew-ins (unless it is linen, see page 29) and then mist the fabric after I have sewn it on; the water shrinks the fabric slightly into the interfacing.

Finally, within subcategories of subcategories, you have specific types of interfacing to do particular jobs – whether it is to add structure, more padding or just gentle support. See, I told you: like a bra! Structure is provided by the strong-arm branch of the family and is great for bags and cap peaks. Padding is what you will need in a quilt; several interfacings can often be layered to get different effects (see also page 49), and sometimes I layer a padding over a structure and attach them both to the fabric to get the best of both worlds. Gentle support interfacing is usually fusible, and it can be used to stop a fraying-prone fabric (like linen or canvas) from fraying, because the glue holds everything together as you cut or sew.

I stick with about six interfacings: H630 (a fusible, light-weight wadding/batting), Style-Vil (a sew-in foam interfacing), S320 (a firm, fusible interfacing – great for pockets), #279 80/20 cotton mix (a sew-in quilting wadding/batting), Decovil and Decovil I Light (two fusible, rigid types of interfacing that are very useful for adding a bit of structure). What's with the weird names? Well, they are all Vlieseline® products and those are the only names that they have; if you search for them online or ask at your favourite sewing shop they are very well known indeed; although if you prefer, you can buy other brands – just make sure you know what type to look for. I will give you more information about all these types in Chapter Two (pages 40–57) and later on in the book too.

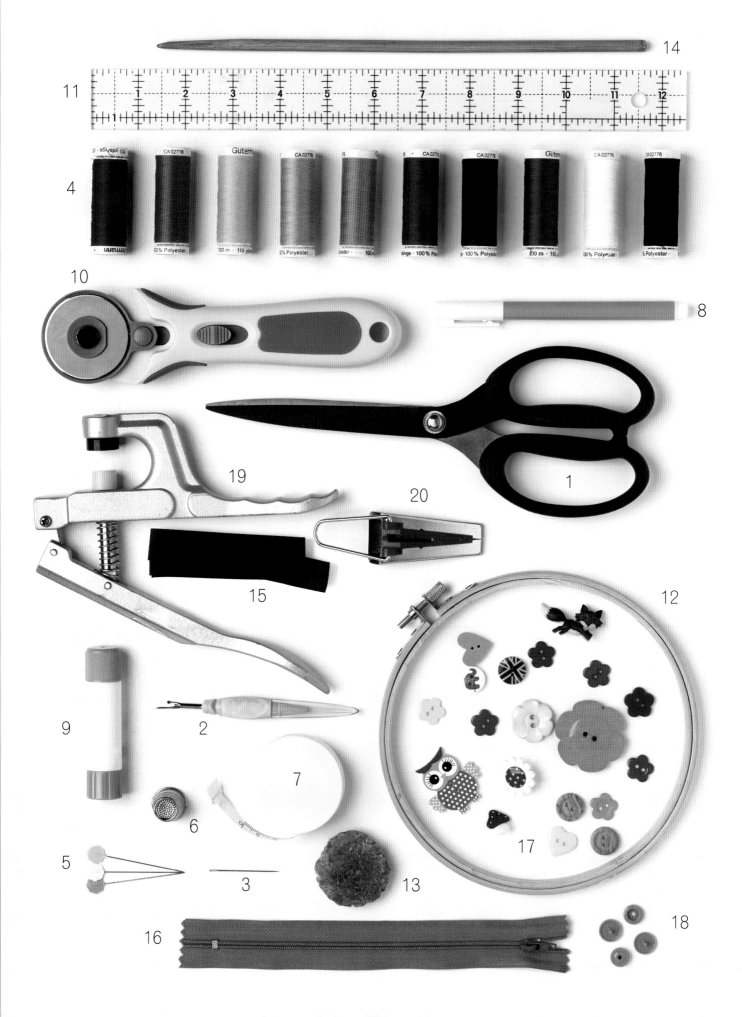

ESSENTIAL SEWING KIT

SEWING MACHINE (NOT SHOWN) You do not need the top-of-the-range machine to begin with – you just need one that will allow you to sew a straight stitch and a zigzag stitch, and a one that can take a couple of different feet. The key three feet to ask about when buying are a walking foot (for quilting), a zip foot (for zips and binding) and a darning foot (for free-motion embroidery, known as FME for short). Don't worry about how to use these at the moment; these special feet will come up as we go. Personally, I love my Janome Memory Craft 8200 QCP Special Edition (you can find this on page 14!) because it does everything. Seriously; I need only this one machine to make everything from a coaster to a king-size quilt.

FABRIC SCISSORS (1) It used to be the case (and there are lots of internet memes about this) that fabric scissors were not to be used for anything other than fabric. Period. On pain of divorce. And in general, this is true. However, a new generation of scissors has emerged: Tonic Studios Tim Holtz Micro-Serrated Scissors. Although they were developed for paper crafters, they can be used for sewing too. Why? These scissors have a special serrated edge on one side that sharpens the blade as it cuts. So, feel free to cut out your fabrics and paper with these at leisure. Tonic Studios Micro-Serrated Scissors come in three sizes – 12.5cm (5in), 17.5cm (7in) and 24cm (9½in). The largest ones (shown here) are a good pair to start with, and are perfect for cutting out your fabric.

QUICK UNPICK/SEAM RIPPER (2)

HAND-SEWING NEEDLES (3) This is a book mainly about machine sewing, but there will be a time for hand-sewing too, mainly to finish off your work. You can find packs of these easily, with five or seven needles inside. Just make sure they're not too long or too small, and the eyes are a reasonable size.

THREAD (4) Thread is an important part of your kit and the best idea is to budget and buy a different coloured reel each time you buy fabric. A plain, good-quality thread is just fine, and as you go along, you can collect more unusual colours. Saying that, you'll be surprised at how few colours you can get away with! I have a mere shoebox-sized collection of thread, yet somehow I can always find one to match my projects. Always try to match the thread to the fabric you use: your work will look instantly better and if your stitching is not yet perfect, a matching thread will hide that fact away from the world.

PINS (5)

THIMBLE (6)

MEASURING TAPE (7)

WATER-SOLUBLE MARKER PEN (8) A modern-day tailor's chalk (although you can still use this), this pen can be used to draw with on fabric; the ink can then be washed out, or will fade in time. Besides drawing outlines, water-soluble marker pens are also perfect for transferring designs. For designs with interfacing,

I advise you to interface your fabric before transferring a design – ideally interface first, draw and cut out second: if you iron over the top of many removable markers (especially the water-soluble ones) you will set them permanently, which is the opposite of useful. When you have a thick fabric like felt (and there'd have to be a nuclear event outside the window before there's strong enough light to see through it), you can draw around your cut-out templates with the pen; these lines will fade over time.

FABRIC GLUE (9) Most fabric glue is just the same as normal glue. As a beginner, you might be tempted to pay more for a branded item but all you really need to have is a non-toxic, water-washable, clear-drying glue. Most white PVA glues will do the trick nicely.

ROTARY CUTTER (10) A rotary cutter should be used with a **SELF-HEALING MAT (NOT SHOWN)** and a **SMALL SEWING RULER (11)**. These are expensive but worth buying for accuracy and also for cutting multiple fabrics at once. If you ever decide to go down the quilting route (and there are some tasty makes later on in the book) this little set will be moved up to the cannot-possibly-live-without category.

EMBROIDERY HOOP (12) This is for hand-sewing, right? Not entirely. Hoops are your best friends when it comes to free-motion embroidery (see Chapter 3, pages 58–73).

WAX BLOCK/THREAD CONDITIONER (13) Bear with me here. It might seem odd to say to you that you need beeswax in your sewing kit. It is not 1830, surely? Well, until you have wrestled (and I am talking knock-down, dragged out fights here) with a piece of thread that is tangling and behaving awfully, you will not see the point. A wax block is used to condition the thread when hand-sewing, stop tangles and make the thread stronger. Your block can even be a lump of old candle, as long as it is colourless and natural beeswax.

CHOPSTICK (14) For turning out narrow projects easily, and gently poking out sewn corners.

HABERDASHERY This section covers **BIAS BINDING (15)** and **BASIC ZIPS (16)** but also accessories and other hardware. The fun stuff begins with **BUTTONS (17)**, and then you can look at **SNAP FASTENERS (18)** (like KAM snaps). When you become more confident, you can play with and invest in metal hardware (see next page). Don't worry about these immediately; I will give proper instructions on how to use them later on.

SNAP PLIERS (19) These are for putting snaps fasteners into projects. They are super easy to use and are specially designed to set the snaps securely into the fabric. Sometimes, they come as part of a kit with snaps included – perfect for beginners.

BIAS TAPE MAKER (20) There's a clue in the name – these are very handy for when you're making your own bias binding. See page 87 for more information on how to use it.

AWL (NOT SHOWN) From the leather industry, this is a handy, cheap tool for punching holes through your fabric for simple hardware. However, it can be prone to tearing the fibres of your fabric a little, so do take care.

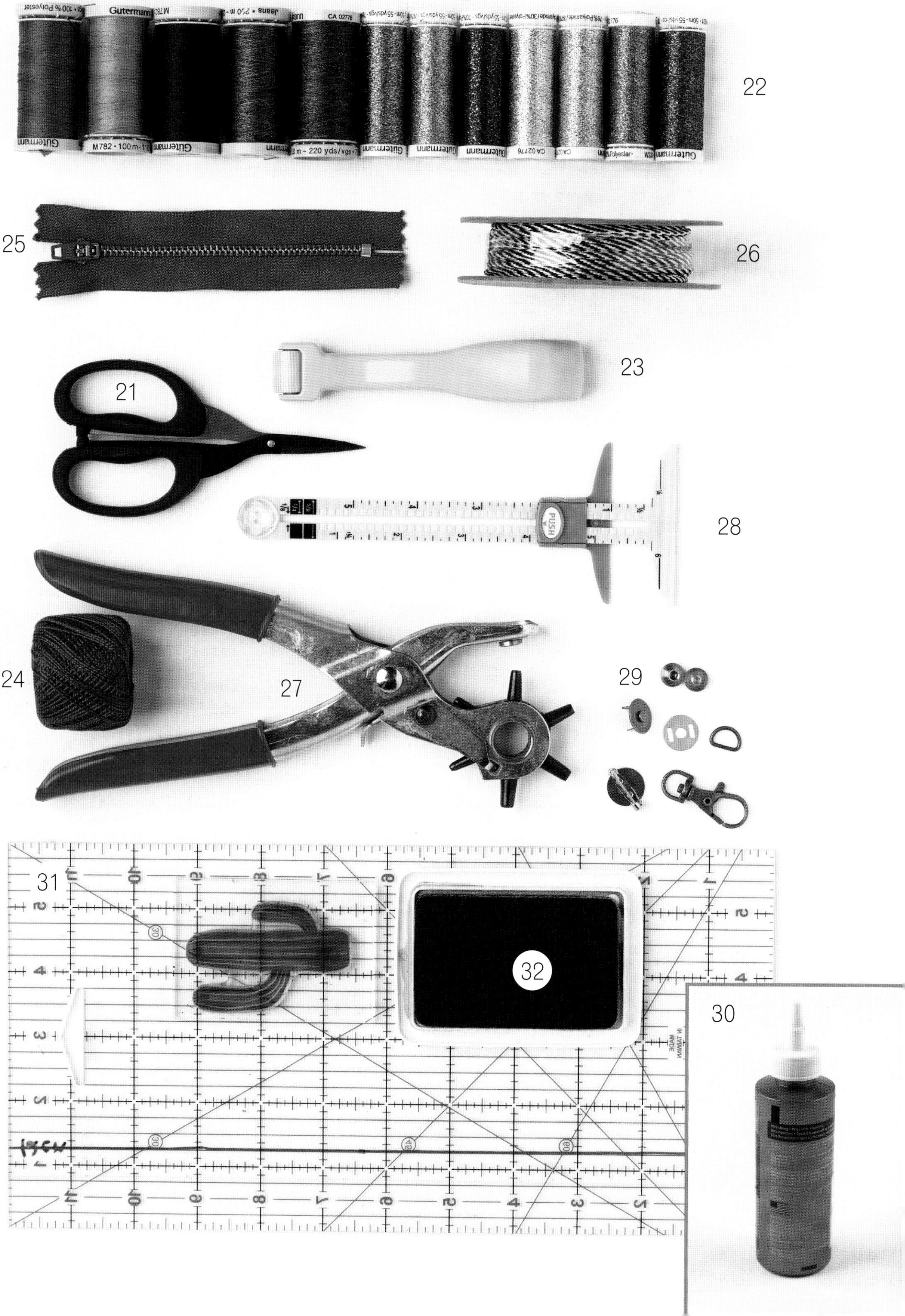

22

25

26

23

21

28

24

27

29

31

32

30

INTERMEDIATE SEWING

When you have got into the swing of sewing, you can add a few more items to your basic kit – let's face it, shopping for 'essentials' is part of the fun! These will appear as you progress through the book. If you don't have them to hand as you begin these sections, alternatives can be used: tools, such as the leather-punch pliers, can be replaced by an awl; patterned twine with regular twine or cord; and binding screws with snap fasteners (see previous page). However, I recommend getting hold of these little extras if you can; not only will they make things a little easier but they will produce the most professional results.

ADDITIONAL SCISSORS (21) Scissors come in all sorts of shapes and sizes, and you can get some specially designed for appliqué with all sorts of strange appearances. But really, all you need in addition to your large pair is a small pair and medium pair. The smallest size is great for snipping thread ends and clipping or notching curved seams (see page 30 for details), the biggest ones are for cutting your fabric out, and the medium size are great for cutting unusual shapes and angles.

SPECIALITY THREADS (22) Not all threads are created equal. Usually, any good-quality thread will do, and you do not need to part with you annual salary to buy a spool of the stuff. It is nice to spend your thread money on the special spools that will add further excitement to your designs. I like to use variegated and metallic threads from Gütermann for fabrics like felt, as their textures work well together, but have a look online and have a look in your local haberdashery store and see what takes your fancy.

SEWING SEAM ROLLER (23)

EMBROIDERY THREAD/FLOSS (24)

METAL ZIP (25) Perfect for heavy-use items that require a stronger zip.

BAKER'S TWINE (26)

REVOLVING LEATHER-PUNCH PLIERS (27) These come from the leather industry; I prefer to use this instead of an awl when punching through fabric as it is more predictable and creates a cleaner hole.

SEWING GAUGE (28) These are special sewing rulers that feature a sliding pointer that moves along a gap in the centre, between the inch and centimetre measurements. They are used mostly in dressmaking to mark hems and pleats accurately, but can be used to draw circles on fabrics too. Simply secure the slide with a pin, place your marker pen in the hole at the end of the ruler then draw away!

METAL HARDWARE (29) Examples include (from top to bottom): metal snap stud/popper, magnetic snap purse clasp, mini D-Ring, brooch back and swivel clasp. Another piece of hardware not included here are binding screws (known also as Chicago screws or sex bolts). Don't worry about what these all are for the moment, if any sound unfamiliar! I will cover them later in the book.

EXTRA-STRONG, ALL-PURPOSE CRAFTING GLUE (30) Perfect for those jobs where appliqué, embellishments or other attachments need to be more secure. Make sure it is clear-drying, so any glue that does seep slightly will be less noticeable.

QUILTING RULER (31) This has lovely straight edges (as you would expect from a ruler!) but its main feature is its thickness. As it is designed to be used with a rotary cutter, it needs to be much thicker than an ordinary ruler: a rotary cutter will cut through a normal ruler and damage the edge (or your fingers – don't ask me how I know). Additionally, the quilting ruler has many useful markings, usually in imperial but sometimes metric, depending on the manufacturer. You can see in the photo where I have made a metric mark on my ruler – you can do this if you prefer this system. There are also angles – all useful for cutting shapes later down the track.

NICE THINGS TO ADD TO THE WISH LIST

Because you have a birthday coming up, it is worth throwing the cap in for some interesting toys which will make your life easier (and more fun).

STAMPS AND INK (32) Yes, seriously! All those times you got a free stamp set with a magazine and wondered what to do with it. Never give them away! I will show you how to make your own, personalized labels with them. You will need ink too, and the one that I really recommend (because I have tested it exhaustively) is Ranger Archival Ink™. It washes well and doesn't fade or smudge.

MANUAL DIE-CUTTING MACHINE (33) Number one on the wish list is a die-cutter. I recommend asking for a Sizzix® Big Shot; I use mine constantly for appliqué and cutting out shapes accurately and quickly. You can do this without one, but when it comes to interesting (not to mention intricate) shapes, you NEED this!

33

SEWING 101

Your sewing machine is your best friend. Carefully chosen, it will last you for years. It is a big investment, so is something to be selected with information behind you. Once you find a favourite, you will likely stick with the brand. Your machine should be able to perform all the basics like straight stitch and zigzag, and ideally it should come with some extra feet – vital for specific details like zip installation and sewing together multiple layers.

Once you gain more experience, it's worth investing in a machine with more features to make your machine sewing even easier. My Janome machine is computerized, with over 200 stitch options, ten buttonhole styles, a long arm (perfect for quilts!) and an automatic needle threader.

ANATOMY OF A SEWING MACHINE

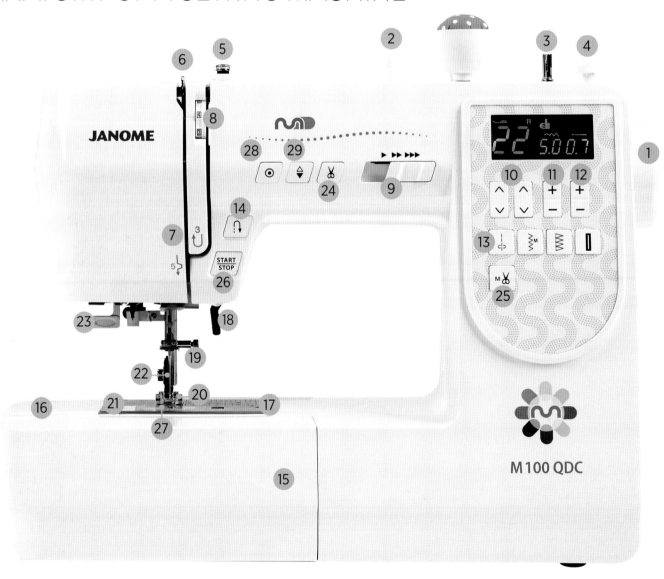

M 100 QDC

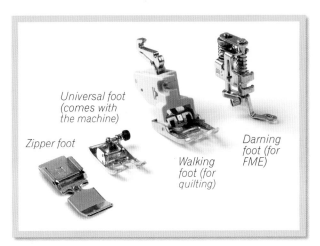

Universal foot
(comes with
the machine)

Zipper foot

Walking
foot (for
quilting)

Darning
foot (for
FME)

FEET

As mentioned earlier, if your first sewing machine doesn't come with extra feet, I recommend that you invest in three more to join the universal foot that comes your machine: zipper foot, walking foot and darning foot. You will not only see how to use each foot as we progress through the book, they will also be invaluable additions to your kit when you tackle your own projects in the future, once you have gained experience and confidence.

1) **HAND WHEEL** – *Sits near the top on the right-hand side of the machine. Turn it to lift or lower the needle. For the model opposite, in conjunction with a switch at the back, it lowers the feed dogs too (see no. 27 below).*

2) **SPOOL HOLDER** – *A long peg for the top thread spool to sit on when sewing.*

3) **BOBBIN WINDER** – *A small peg for the bobbin to sit on, to wind thread onto it in preparation for sewing. (See the lingo box also on page 17.)*

4) **BOBBIN WINDER STOP** – *A built in device on some machines that stops the bobbin winding automatically when it is full.*

5) **BOBBIN WINDING TENSION DISC** – *The thread from the spool runs around this when preparing its tension.*

6) **THREAD TAKE-UP LEVER** – *The thread from the tension control hooks around this to maintain tension.*

7) **THREAD GUIDE** – *The thread from the tension control wraps around this curve to keep your thread in place as you sew.*

8) **TENSION CONTROL** – *Varies from machine to machine, especially on digital ones. This dial controls the tension of the top thread on the spool. The smaller the number, the greater the tension, and vice versa.*

9) **SPEED CONTROL** – *Is what it is!*

10) **STITCH SELECTOR** – *The arrows allow you to select a number which represents different stitches.*

11) **STITCH WIDTH** – *Increases or decreases the width of the stitch. Used mostly for decorative stitches like zigzag stitch.*

12) **STITCH LENGTH** – *Increases or decreases the length of the stitch. This is important for sewing, as the stitch lengths a fabric will take varies with each type. If a stitch is too short, it can pucker the fabric. If the stitch is too long, the seam will not hold together properly.*

13) **DIRECT PATTERN SELECTION** – *To quickly select commonly used stitches. These tend to include more specialized stitches, such as buttonholes.*

14) **REVERSE STITCH** – *Can be a button or lever, depending on the machine. Allows you to reverse stitch, which you can use to manually reverse over previous stitches and secure your stitching before continuing to sew, or cutting the thread.*

15) **REMOVABLE ACCESSORY COMPARTMENT** – *Slides off to reveal a hidden compartment for sewing-machine accessories; also allows you to reveal the 'free arm', making it smaller and therefore easier to sew sleeves, for example.*

16) **SEWING MACHINE 'FREE ARM'** – *When revealed, is handy for sewing tubular shapes. Removing the case also allows you on some models (such as the Janome model, right) to attach a special sewing table, ideal for large projects.*

17) **NEEDLE/THROAT PLATE** – *Often includes handy measurements for seam allowances.*

18) **PRESSER FOOT LEVER** – *Sits behind the needle, raises or lowers the foot.*

19) **NEEDLE CLAMP** – *Loosen or tighten to remove and swap to another needle.*

20) **PRESSER FOOT** – *Universal shown. Can be removed easily to change to another foot.*

21) **BOBBIN COMPARTMENT** – *Placement varies with each machine; this is a top-loading one. (See the lingo box on page 17.)*

22) **NEEDLE** – *Change this when it blunts, or if switching to a particular fabric.*

23) **PULL DOWN SELF-THREADING BUTTON** – *Appears mostly on high-end machines, and is very useful if you find the threading process tricky.*

24) **AUTO THREAD CUTTER** – *Most machines include a blade on the side of the machine that you can use to cut the thread, once you've finish stitching. Computerized models, such as this one, come with an automatic thread cutter, too, that cuts the thread automatically under the bobbin area, allowing you to release your work quickly.*

25) **THREAD CUT MEMORY KEY** – *Appears on some digital machines, this is programmed to cut the thread automatically at the end of your memorized stitch selection.*

26) **START/STOP BUTTON** – *On computerized machines this button can control the machine without the need for a plug-in foot pedal. The plug-in foot control is operated in a similar way to driving a car. This particular model features both, to suit the preference of the sewist.*

27) **FEED DOGS** – *Sit just below the presser foot, within the needle/throat plate. Can be raised or lowered for FME (see Chapter 3, page 59.*

28) **LOCK STITCH** – *Features on some digital machines, this button allows you to sew tiny stitches in the same spot when making straight or zigzag stitches, or other common stitches. Lock stitches are useful when sewing decorative stitches especially, which would be spoilt by regular reverse stitching. For decorative stitches, the lock stitch is made once the final shape is stitched.*

29) **NEEDLE UP/DOWN BUTTON** – *Appears on some models; press to bring the needle up or down quickly.*

Some machines include sewing tables – perfect for large projects such as quilts.

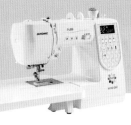

Sewing is about joining pieces of fabric together – in this book, we are doing this with a sewing machine. Every project in this book has been designed so you learn a few machine-sewing techniques with each one, that you can then build on over the subsequent projects. We will put these sewing skills into practice very soon but first, let's take a look at the key things about sewing that are important to know, before you jump onto your machine!

ANATOMY OF FABRIC

Woven fabric is made by weaving long, fine threads or yarn together. The ones that go up and down are known as **warp** threads, and the ones that run to the left and right are called **weft** threads. These interlace to create a **grain**. The **straight grain** therefore runs two ways – up and down, and across the fabric (sometimes know as the **cross grain**).

The straight grain has no stretch. Find a fat quarter (FQ) you've just bought and pull the fabric these ways to test it. See how it barely moves? Now pull the FQ diagonally, from each corner. See how it stretches a little? Here, we have something called the **bias**. You will see how this works later on, as you go through the projects in this book. Since the bias grain has a slight stretch, it can have a habit of warping and buckling, so you do have to be careful with it when you cut it out and sew with it. However, you can use the stretchiness of bias-cut fabric to your advantage. More on that later too.

Unless stated otherwise (in the pattern or on the template), fabric should be cut on the straight grain.

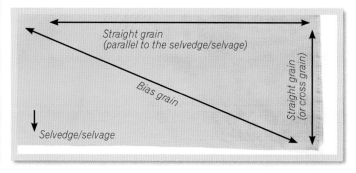

THERE ARE TWO SIDES TO EVERY FABRIC

First things first. Look at your fabric and turn it over. Can you see that one side is nicer than the other? The nice side is known as the 'right side' and the other side is the 'wrong side'.

You will often see in a pattern the instruction to 'place the right sides together'. That means to put the fabric together with the two nicest sides touching. You deliberately sew these nice sides together so that when the item is turned out the right way, the fabric will be the right way out and the seams will be hidden. Occasionally, this is different (such as when quilting and patching – see Chapter 4, pages 78–99), but the usual rule is to sew right sides together.

MEASURING YOUR FABRIC ACCURATELY

No measuring is possible without having a very straight edge. Usually, sewists use the **selvedge/selvage** to help them measure, as this is the straightest edge (see also 'Anatomy of Fabric' opposite). The selvedge/selvage is the edge of the fabric that is 'self-finished', meaning it has been industrially hemmed or bound with bias tape to prevent the fabric from fraying. The easiest way to spot it is that it is often either the edge with the information about the fabric printed on it, which runs down the whole length of the fabric, or the edge that is perforated.

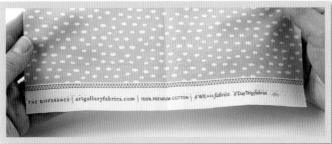

Selvedge/selvage. Look out for a 'self-finished' edge; sometimes this has the fabric information on it, too.

A number of the projects you will sew in this book are made from fat quarters (FQs). Sometimes, you may not find a selvedge/selvage edge on a FQ and, more often, you will find your FQs are not perfectly cut. You will need to straighten its edges by trimming them with your ruler and rotary cutter (the best way), or with fabric scissors along a ruled line (not so good but possible).

READING A PATTERN

Pattern instructions are often simplified and assume you know the necessary sewing techniques, so you are likely to find terms or methods that are not well explained. Throughout the book, I have a 'Sewing 101' introduction that will hopefully fill in the gaps that most sewing patterns have left out. Then, as you continue to sew, you will soon get a feel for what to do and how to do it.

Sewing patterns often come in two forms: sometimes there will be written instructions only, other times templates or diagrams will be included on a paper or on a separate sheet. If there is a template, cut it out first, pin it to the fabric and then cut the shape out following the edge of the template – just as you would for a drawing or a 'normal' paper pattern for dressmaking.

SETTING UP FOR SEWING

Although the essential sewing-machine features have been covered on the previous pages, it is beyond the scope of any book to go through the ins and outs of your sewing machine because they are all different. For this reason, do have a look at your machine's manual before you start sewing, and search online for some videos on your specific brand to master the basics. Throughout the projects, I will assume you have filled a bobbin and threaded up the sewing machine, and have inserted a universal foot onto your machine (if it isn't in place already!). Again, do look through your machine's manual carefully, as each one will have a particular way to prepare your top thread and bobbin, and securing your universal foot.

When your fabric is secured (by pinning or tacking/basting) and you're ready to go, lay your fabric on the needle plate so that the needle above sits 5mm (¼in) from the edge. This distance between the needle and edge is called the **seam allowance**, and this not only helps the seam you make stay neat, it keeps it away from the raw edge of the fabric, which can fray and unravel. Unless stated otherwise in the pattern, a 5mm (¼in) seam allowance should be used every time you sew.

LINGO: 'BOBBIN'

This is a small, cylindrical spindle that fits into your machine under the needle plate, and which the 'bottom' thread is wound around. When in motion, the machine's threaded needle (which uses the 'top' thread) catches the thread in this bobbin, and combined they allow the sewing machine to make a stitch.

 Sometimes you will need to join two pieces of different coloured fabric, and that means that you will have one colour thread in the top of the machine and a different colour in the bobbin. That is absolutely fine: just make sure that your tension is correct (the standard factory setting on your sewing machine is usually fine), and you will not see either thread from the side where it shouldn't be.

Seam allowance, 5mm (¼in) from the edge.

THE PROJECTS

Well, we're ready to start machine sewing! Before you dive in, it's worth taking note of how to approach the projects and information in this book.

HOW TO READ THIS BOOK

◎ Each new project starts with a 'Sewing 101' – this is a summary of what you'll be learning in the particular project before you start sewing, as well as other useful information worth knowing before you begin.

◎ The main 'Pattern' follows next. This is laid out in a more conventional sewing-pattern format, and will help you get familiar with how to read and understand sewing instructions.

◎ This is a progressive sewing book, and my hope is you gain experience (and confidence) with every new thing you sew! With each new item, you should need less explanation for the more familiar techniques. However, if you do need to remind yourself of a particular method, I will provide you with a page reference. Do refer to the index at the back of the book too!

> **TIP**
> White 'Tip' boxes give extra advice for working a particular step, or offer fun alternatives you could try.

TECHNIQUES
Grey 'Techniques' boxes detail techniques, as well as other useful know-how.

LINGO:
Coloured 'Lingo' boxes explain sewing terms.

QUILTING COTTON ————

Neck Pillow

PATTERN

Now we are ready to have a look at a simple pattern. Always ensure that you have all of the materials assembled before you begin, and read through the instructions carefully so that there are no nasty surprises.

Our first pattern requires one fat quarter (FQ) of patterned fabric, and a fat eighth (F8th) of a darker solid fabric for lettering. In addition, only two rectangles of fabric are needed to make this pillow, so you don't need a template. All you have to do is to cut your FQ fabric to the sizes directed in the pattern (see page 22), pin the two pieces right sides together and sew along the edges. You will be working on the straight grain of the fabric; this means that this project is easy to sew, with no worries about stretching and distorting.

The pillow has some pretty details and these are as easy as pie to make. The first detail is the word 'ahhhh' cut from the dark solid F8th, and the second is a little ribbon tab. You can choose to leave out these features if you wish, but they will lift your make to internet-worthy. For the letters, I recommend a die-cutter and die, but you could use a large, unfussy downloadable font and fabric scissors.

WHAT YOU WILL LEARN:

- Reading a simple pattern
- Working with fabric on a straight grain
- Sewing a straight stitch
- Sewing in a straight line
- Sewing around a right-angled corner
- Making a sharp corner in your fabric
- Making and closing a turning gap
- Reducing bulk
- Adding details

GATHER THESE SUPPLIES:

- Fabric
  - FQ mustard yellow quilting cotton
  - F8th solid fabric, in a colour to contrast with the main fabric: mine is black
- Rice or other filling, for stuffing
- Your essential sewing kit (see page 11)
- Optional: ribbon, manual die-cutting machine plus alphabet dies

LINGO: 'SOLID'

Hang on, so what is a **solid**? Good question! When talking about fabric, a solid means that it doesn't have a pattern on it. 'Plain' is another word to describe it, but in the sewing world you will see the word solid more often.

1 Using the solid fabric, cut out your letters using fabric scissors and printed letters (or die-cutting machine and alphabet dies). You need at least one 'A' and four 'H's.

DIE-CUTTING

If you are working with a fabric that has a definite right and wrong side, place the fabric onto the die with the wrong side facing down, so that the letters will be the right way up when you cut them out (not mirror image). On a solid (or 'plain') fabric, you don't need to worry about this as there's no 'right side' as such.

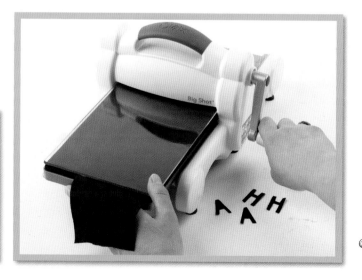

2 On the back (wrong side) of your FQ, measure out your two rectangles, 12 x 56cm (4¾x 22in) and cut them out on the straight grain – you'll notice the longest edge of the FQ is exactly 56cm (22in), so use this to your advantage! If your fabric is shorter, don't worry – just make your pillow shorter too! On one rectangle (which will become the front), arrange the letters to make the word 'ahhhh'. Glue them down with fabric glue when you are happy with the placement.

CUTTING OUT FABRIC

The golden rule when cutting your fabric out is to measure twice and cut once!

3 Trim the ribbon, if needed, to a 5cm (2in) length and fold it in half to make a small loop. Attach this to the right-hand end of the rectangular panel.

TIP

If you wish, you can make this loop longer so that it is a fully functioning hanging loop, instead of just a bit of decoration.

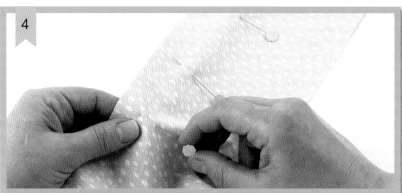

4 With the right sides together, pin the second panel to your embellished panel.

TIP

Place your pins so they sit horizontally to the seam. This makes it easier to pull them out when your fabric is in the machine.

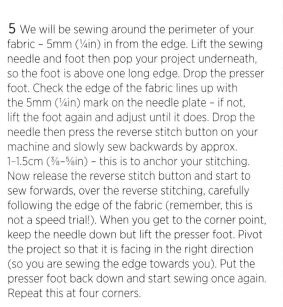

5 We will be sewing around the perimeter of your fabric – 5mm (¼in) in from the edge. Lift the sewing needle and foot then pop your project underneath, so the foot is above one long edge. Drop the presser foot. Check the edge of the fabric lines up with the 5mm (¼in) mark on the needle plate – if not, lift the foot again and adjust until it does. Drop the needle then press the reverse stitch button on your machine and slowly sew backwards by approx. 1–1.5cm (⅜–⅝in) – this is to anchor your stitching. Now release the reverse stitch button and start to sew forwards, over the reverse stitching, carefully following the edge of the fabric (remember, this is not a speed trial!). When you get to the corner point, keep the needle down but lift the presser foot. Pivot the project so that it is facing in the right direction (so you are sewing the edge towards you). Put the presser foot back down and start sewing once again. Repeat this at four corners.

SEWING SPEED

Try not to sew too fast or slow. Sewing is a bit like riding a bike: some momentum is necessary to sew straight. Keep practising and it will start to feel natural.

6 Don't sew the last long edge completely; leave a gap of about 5cm (2in) away. This is your turning gap. This gap will allow you to turn your project the right way out. Reverse stitch in the same way as before, then lift the presser foot and needle. Gently pull your sewing away from the machine and cut the threads on both sides of the fabric.

7 Before we turn the project out, we have to clip across the corners. This is done to reduce bulk when the project is turned the right way out. Simply snip across the corner, but take care you don't do it too close to the stitching, or it will come undone. Repeat for all of the corners.

8 Turn the pillow the right way out through the turning gap. Now you will notice that the corners are not sharp. We need to do something about this! So let's look at a new, very high-tech piece of kit... It's called a chopstick! Gently poke the corners out until they are 'sharp'.

9 Fill your bag about two-thirds full with rice and close the gap by machine, using a regular straight stitch. To make this close extra secure, sew backwards and forwards a few times over your sewn seam.

HAND-SEWING A GAP CLOSED

If you like hand-sewing, you can close up the gap by hand. This produces a neater result, as you can't see the stitching. See page 31 to find out how.

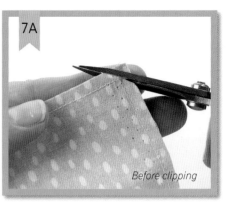

Before clipping

After clipping

And look at you! You now have some basic machine-sewing skills and have produced something that is practical and usable.

If not, don't be disheartened; it is just down to practice. If you are less than happy with a result, you can simply unpick it and do it again. There are actually only two sorts of sewists in the world – those who admit to unpicking, and the liars. Really. We all start by giving our quick unpick a thorough workout. So if that is you, it is not a failure but an entrée to the club. Welcome!

Coasters

Felt is not just for children to play with! The good stuff (wool or wool mix) is wonderfully warm and tactile and cannot fray. Seriously. No finishing of edges is necessary because of this (always worth celebrating as a new machine sewist), which opens it up for all sorts of uses.

WHAT YOU WILL LEARN:

◉ All about felt
◉ All about leather
◉ Fabric glues
◉ Top-stitching

SEWING 101

All about felt

Felt is made by meshing fibres together with barbed needles (dry felting) or heat and water (wet felting). Friction and heat causes the fibres to tangle and enmesh for good (remember the time that you put a pure wool jumper into a too-hot cycle and it came out fit for a four year old?). Felting is permanent – you cannot comb dreadlocks out, and this is the same principle. This gives us a sturdy fibre with no grain, which is the reason why it cannot fray – it is not woven.

Felt is suitable for sewing and die-cutting, and whenever you work with it always save the scraps because it is very suitable for appliqué too. Since felt comes in a range of thicknesses, it is useful for a variety of things: really thin felt is great for regular sewing – working just as you would with 'normal' fabric, and thicker felt is perfect for slipper soles (or even slippers themselves). For this project, you need something a little more substantial – at least 2.5–3mm (approx. ⅛in) thick.

Because felt is non-woven, you can cut your fabric pieces exactly to size, without the need for trimming or leaving seam allowances. This means less waste too!

All about leather

Leather is fun to work with and will give your makes an instant lift! Leather cuts well with a rotary cutter, and most home sewing machines will handle it well. The coaster pattern has some little leather tabs on the side of each coaster and, as you can see, it gives them a lovely modern effect.

Most of the time, you can use a universal needle to sew leather scraps like these, and it follows the usual rule for machine sewing fabrics – the thicker the fabric, the larger the needle. However, do consider buying a packet of leather needles for your sewing machine, especially if you are going to use leather a lot and in much larger cuts. Universal machine needles can 'cut' through the fabric too much, and distort or damage the leather. Leather needles prevent this.

DENIM NEEDLES

While we're on the subject of special needles, you can also buy special needles for denim. While the universal needle is an enemy to leather, because it's too aggressive for the fabric, the exact opposite is the case for denim – the fabric is too thick for the needle, and will damage it! Again, I recommend buying a pack of these needles only if you intend to start sewing with large cuts of denim. Some of the makes in this book feature denim-like cotton fabrics, and these are perfect for beginner sewists who want the look for their homewares or accessories, but don't need to change (or have the fear of breaking) the needle!

PATTERN

So! I reckon that we are just about ready for another pattern. This time, it is a set of very useful coasters. You can either die-cut them for perfect circles or use the templates provided on Pattern Sheet B. They are then simply glued together and top-stitched. This pattern makes four coasters.

GATHER THESE SUPPLIES:

- Fabric
  - Two pieces of felt, each approx. 30cm (12in) square: make these contrasting colours – I have chosen a heathered grey and a mustard
- Strip of tan leather, 10 x 1.5cm (4 x ⅝in)
- Your essential sewing kit (see page 11)
- Optional: manual die-cutting machine plus two circular dies – 7.5cm (3in) and 10cm (4in) in diameter

TEMPLATES ON PATTERN SHEET B

1 Begin by cutting four smaller circles from the mustard felt with the 7.5cm (3in) template or die, and four larger ones from the grey felt with the 10cm (4in) template or die.

2 Take your 10 x 1.5cm (4 x ⅝in) strip of leather and subcut it into four equal pieces, 2.5cm (1in) long.

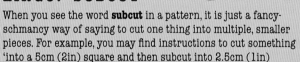

LINGO: 'SUBCUT'

When you see the word **subcut** in a pattern, it is just a fancy-schmancy way of saying to cut one thing into multiple, smaller pieces. For example, you may find instructions to cut something 'into a 5cm (2in) square and then subcut into 2.5cm (1in) pieces'. It just means to cut again.

3 Take one of the larger grey circles and glue a smaller mustard one centrally to the top of it. Tuck a leather tab under the edge somewhere – because the coaster is round, it doesn't matter where you put the tab but make sure that the end is tucked well under, so that it will be caught in the top-stitching

FABRIC GLUES

The clear drying aspect of fabric glue is important here, because if you do smudge it a bit, you really don't want to be able to see it. This is important for all your makes that involve a little gluing, as it will leave you with a professional finish.

4 Once the leather tab is secured in place, trim it down to match the edge of the grey felt. Try to round the edge of the leather as you cut, to match the curve of the felt.

5 Top-stitch around the edge of the smaller circle, 5mm (¼in) in from the edge. To do this, just follow the edge of the top circle with your presser foot to keep the stitching on track.

6 Repeat for the other coasters.

TOP-STITCHING

It's fun to break the rules now and then! Occasionally, you will want the stitching to be visible and a part of the design. (Note: this is rarely the case for stitching normal seams; here, you want the stitching to be invisible). **Top-stitching** is different from regular stitching as it can be a functional or decorative stitch, or both. It is functional, for example, where you are sewing in a zip or on the top of a bag and you want the lining to stay down – top-stitching will get this job done. However, because you also see it and therefore might like to make it decorative, you can use a thread to make these stitches stand out more and emphasize the sewn feature. Finally, you might use top-stitching for show, as you often see on denim jeans. It has the added benefit of giving strength, too.

So far, we have worked with nice fabrics which don't mean you any harm. Cue demonic laughter. This time, I want to talk about linen.

Now, why is this the evil cousin of cotton? Because it creases (a lot) and it frays (and seems like it has nothing else better to do). Unfortunately for you, it is also worth its weight in terms of style, so it is a good idea to learn how to use it.

WHAT YOU WILL LEARN:

- About linen
- Sewing curves
- Notching a seam
- Hand-sewing 'invisible' stitches (just a bit, I promise!)
- Functional embellishment

SEWING 101

About linen

Linen is a woven fabric. It has threads going up and down (warp) and across (weft), and a grain like the quilting cotton from the first project. But linen is woven a lot more loosely than quilting cotton, therefore it is just waiting to fray.

There are two ways of combatting this. You can use pinking shears (a special kind of scissors with a saw-toothed, zigzag blade), or you can cut your project larger and slightly increase your seam allowance so that the thread has something to bite into. Personally, I don't like to use pinking shears as I find the blades pull on the fabric too much, so I tend to go for the other option. So how much extra fabric in the seam are we talking here? A 'normal' seam allowance is 5mm (¼in). To avoid using numbers, some patterns will say to take a 'generous ¼in', which simply means the usual amount plus a little bit extra. As this extra measurement is only a whisker, it will not make too much difference to the finished size of the make – especially if it is not clothing. So, just position your sewing needle just a little wider than usual and that should suffice.

If you find that linen (or other loose-woven fabric) still frays too much, you can use a light-weight fusible interfacing on the wrong side to help stabilize it. In addition, I find that reducing my stitch length helps a lot too. Reducing the stitch length makes the stitches tighter, and this allows them to grab onto the fabric weave tightly; the weave then cannot 'wiggle out' and fray. You do not have to reduce the stitch length very much – go with whatever is factory set as normal on your particular machine first then reduce it by a couple of increments. Practise on a scrap piece of fabric initially to see what is right for your sewing machine and your linen. To find out how to reduce your stitch length on your machine, consult your machine's manual (or see 'Anatomy of A Sewing Machine' on page 14).

As for tackling the creasing, I can tell you confidently that you could iron linen all day and the creases are likely to just laugh at you. Instead, mist them first with a normal spray bottle and cold water; this makes them relax and melt away. Then, when you iron, you have a much greater chance of ending up with a flat piece of fabric – this is especially important when cutting out your fabric.

Linen has one more trick up its sleeve too: it shrinks the first time you wet it (I know, you are probably asking yourself why you should bother). Again, misting the fabric first, before cutting out, will help you tackle this issue: misting preshrinks the linen so

it should not shrink again. Misting also meshes the fibres together slightly, like felting, and reduces the risk of fraying. For this reason, I would advise misting the fabric before you begin, even if there are no real creases. If your linen creases again (especially after turning your stitched project out the right way), blast it again with a fine mist.

Sewing curves

Round sewing is scary right? Wrong! Oh, and by the way, you have already done it but I didn't want to say... Last chapter's top-stitching was actually sewing a curve. Just sayin'.

To sew a curve is as easy as sewing straight; all you have to do is follow the curve with your presser foot carefully, steering the fabric with both hands as the needle moves. It is as simple as that. Have a practice on some scrap fabric first, if you like.

Hand-sewing 'invisible' stitches

Before we start, I should let you know there is a little bit of hand-sewing in this project. In the first project (pages 20–23) we closed the turning gap by machine, but it did leave a noticeable line. Another way to close a gap is with ladder stitch, and this is what we'll be doing with your pincushion. Ladder stitch will allow you to close the gap invisibly. We'll have a look at the technique for this in greater detail in the pattern.

Functional embellishment

I should have waited for the chapter on haberdashery (see pages 100–119), but I could not leave it any longer to tell you to collect buttons! Just about everyone can remember playing with an elderly relative's button box at some point in their childhood. I don't know what it is about buttons, but they are über addictive. Well, the good news is that they are one childhood joy that you don't have to leave behind. Collect buttons in all shapes, sizes and materials. Our pincushion has two, one on top and one on the bottom (not shown), and they serve both a functional and decorative purpose. The two together draw in the cushion on either side – helping to distribute the tension needed to give the pincushion shape – and stop the stitches from pulling right out. The 'top' button also acts as a centre for the flower, and the bottom one helps to balance the design and make the cushion look pretty too.

PATTERN

PRESSING THE FABRIC BEFORE SEWING

Although you often use an iron for pressing, it is worth pointing out that there is a world of difference between 'ironing' and 'pressing'. Ironing is where you put the iron down on the fabric and move it back and forth – the sort of motion that you associate with ironing clothing. You can't do this with items you're sewing – or about to sew – because this can create distortion in the fabric and bend it out of shape, especially if there are bias edges. Pressing, on the other hand, is the action of bringing the iron straight down and then lifting it up again without moving it back and forth. This delivers heat and the weight of the iron to flatten the fabric in preparation for sewing, to set a seam or to make a crease, but does not carry the same 'danger' of pulling the fabric out of shape.

1 Preshrink and press the linen.

2 Cut two circles, one from linen and the other from floral fabric, using the template on Pattern Sheet B.

3 With the right sides together, sew around the edge using a generous 5mm (¼in) seam allowance. Leave a turning gap just large enough to turn the pincushion out – about 4cm (1½in) is perfect. Make sure to reverse stitch on either side of the gap.

4 As the pincushion is round, it will need to have its curves 'notched' before it can be turned out the right way. This is a simple matter of using sharp scissors to cut little 'Vs' into the seam allowance, being very careful not to cut the stitching.

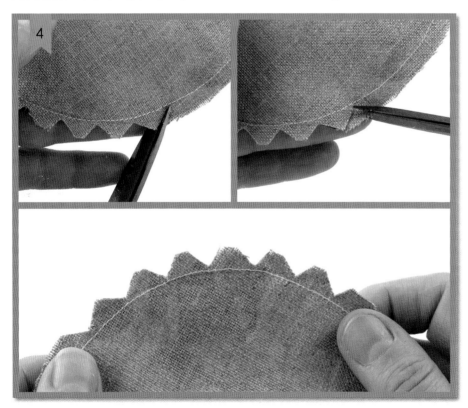

5 Turn the pincushion the right way out and gently manipulate the sides so that they are neat. Stuff well with polyester stuffing/fibrefill.

GATHER THESE SUPPLIES:

- Fabric
  - 30cm (12in) square piece of natural linen
  - 30cm (12in) square piece of floral quilting cotton
  - Piece of red leather, approx. 20cm (8in) square
- Two small wooden buttons
- Strong sewing thread
- Polyester stuffing/fibrefill
- Your essential sewing kit (see page 11)
- Optional: manual die-cutting machine plus flower dies

TEMPLATES ON PATTERN SHEET B

TIP

Stitching in a circle can be a bit scary! To help, draw a circle on to your fabric first with a water-soluble marker pen; you can then follow this as you sew. Once you're finished, remove the pen marks with a cotton bud/swab (see Step 6 on page 43 for help).

WHY NOTCH?

What this does is makes a bit more room in the seam allowance by literally removing some of the fabric. When the project is turned the right way out, these little 'V's will nestle together and stop the edges of the fabric from puckering and distorting. This is the usual practice for rounded edges in sewing, so whenever you get a round bit on a pattern, you should notch the curves.

I love the small-sized Tonic Studios Micro-Serrated scissors for this job. They are unbelievably accurate and can handle any fabric. You can use a large pair of fabric scissors to do this, but smaller scissors will make your life easier.

6 Now you're ready to close the gap with ladder stitch. Begin by knotting the end of your thread and strengthening it with wax.

7 Anchor the thread in one end of the gap by taking the needle up from the wrong side through to the top of the fabric. Finger press a seam allowance on the other side of the gap, on the other fabric piece, so that you can see where to sew and create a folded line to work along. Now, make a tiny stitch along the edge of this new fold [**A**]. Make sure your new stitch is parallel to the fold. Take the needle across to the other side of the gap and make a tiny stitch in the same way as before, approx. 5mm (¼in) further than the previous stitch [**B**]. Keep doing this until you reach the end of the gap [**C**]. You can see why it is called ladder stitch!

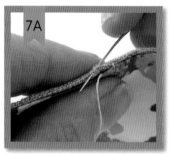

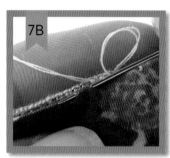

From one side...   *... to the other.*

LINGO:
'FINGER PRESSING'

Finger pressing or **finger creasing** is a way to get a crease without the permanence of ironing. You simply run your finger (or better still, your nail) along the part that you want to crease, and that is usually enough to make a mark. A sewing seam roller (see pages 12–13, number 22) makes this process a little quicker and will also put less strain on your nails!

Several worked ladder stitches.

TIP

Sewing reverse stitch earlier on either side of the turning gap will strengthen the edges of your ladder stitches.

8 Cut a couple of flowers from leather using the die or the flower templates on Pattern Sheet B. With a strong hand needle, sew the buttoned flower to the top and a button on the bottom. Begin by sewing the back button on once or twice and then add the flower and the other button on top.

9 Finish by gently drawing the cushion together in the centre by passing the needle right through the cushion and going through both buttons. This may be fiddly at first, but will leave you with a neat finish.

TIP

If you'd like to make a smaller or larger pincushion, either draw around a circular item that you'd like the size of your cushion to be, or use a sewing gauge (see pages 10 and 11). Remember to include the generous seam allowance!

Dog Chew Toy

The pattern this time is for a dog toy – because it is a bone shape, we have a great opportunity to study tighter curves and also talk more about clipping and notching (don't worry – I'll explain what 'clipping' is in a moment!). In addition, last time we looked at linen. This time, I want you to see how canvas compares to it.

WHAT YOU WILL LEARN:

◎ About canvas
◎ Sewing sharper curves
◎ Clipping a seam
◎ Stamping and top-stitching a label

SEWING 101

About canvas

Like linen, canvas is a loosely woven material and therefore inclined to fray, so in most cases I treat linen and canvas in the same way. But, like linen, it is worth getting to know canvas a little better: it is a wonderfully strong fabric – a Herculean version of linen – making it suitable for a myriad of uses, especially in homewares and bag making. Because it is so sturdy, it does not need much in the way of interfacing (more about that later). In addition, canvas doesn't need to be preshrunk and will not react to water in the same way that linen does; this means you can use it like regular fabric. However, remember that canvas is prone to fraying so do treat the edges with respect.

Some of the modern prints available on canvas are just lush, so if the qualities above haven't won you over yet, it is worth exploring in store or online to see what's available.

Sewing sharper curves

So far, you have managed to negotiate a nice gentle curve on the pincushion. There were no real direction changes. With a bone shape, we have a straight bit and then two funny shaped ends.

There are two tricks to sewing these. The first thing is to go slowly. The second is to lift and drop the presser foot: sew until you get to a bit where there is a direction change then come to a stop with the needle down. Lift the presser foot, gently turn the project, drop the presser foot again and then continue until the next change of direction.

And that is actually the only thing to know about sewing a tighter curve! When you finish negotiating the tighter curve, it's important to put that presser foot back down again, as you still need to allow it to follow the edge of the fabric shape.

Clipping

Our bone shape will need to be notched on the rounded ends, like the pincushion, but there are a few more 'pulling points' on the fabric which will need some attention too. At the end of each straight bit, just before the main curve starts, there is a major direction change – a concave. Shapes like these in fabric need to be 'clipped' into. **Clipping** is the close relative of notching. It releases the tension in the fabric and allows it to stretch out around the corner (see page 35). Once the bone is turned out the right way, you will have a lovely neat corner.

Stamping and top-stitching a label

Now a bit of fun to cool down with, before we make a start. I have always loved finding new uses for things, especially crafting gear, and I especially love the free stamps that come with magazines. These are useless unless you make cards, right? Wrong! We sewists can use them to make things too! I love to use them to make labels for my makes, which I then top-stitch on or add into the seam.

For the main label, you can use faux leather but I cannot guarantee how the results will turn out. If you prefer not to use leather, choose paper fabric Kraft-Tex® paper instead. This is nice to stamp and sew with and is a washable product, perfect for an item that will need a lot of washing! A selection of die shapes in ovals and circles are handy for cutting out your labels, but they are not essential.

You will also need an ink pad and, of course, you need stamps. Choose a stamp without too many details; although these will print happily on paper and other similar things, more complicated designs will not transfer as well. My favourite brand of ink is Ranger Archival Ink™. It doesn't fade, and the things I have stamped with it have been through the washing machine several times with no ill effects.

PATTERN

1 Cut the bone shape out from your canvas twice using the template on Pattern Sheet B.

2 To make the leather label for your bone, cut a square from the scrap of leather 3cm (1¼in) in size (or use a small square die), and stamp it with your chosen stamp.

3 Position the label on the right side of one bone piece (this will become the 'front'), well in from the edges, and secure in place with a spot of glue. You can use the full-sized picture on page 32 as a guide, if you wish. Top-stitch the label on with the denim thread.

4 Place the bone pieces right sides together and stitch around the outer edge with a generous 5mm (¼in) seam allowance, leaving a turning gap on one straight side.

A BIT MORE ABOUT TURNING GAPS

- Sometimes they're known as **stuffing gaps**, but most of the time a pattern will refer to them as turning gaps.
- As a golden rule, always leave the turning gap on a straight bit of fabric if you can. On the pincushion before (see pages 28–31), we had no choice; the whole thing was round so the gap had to be left on the curve.
- The size of the gap will depend on what you are turning. Ideally, they are made as small as possible to cut down on hand-sewing, but it shouldn't be too small else you'll stretch the gap or worse – tear it. Experience will teach you how big it should be.

5 Now for the notching and clipping. To clip, use those perfect little scissors once again and make one cut right up to (but not into) the stitching line. Repeat this in the three remaining inner corners. Once the bone is turned out the right way, you will see that you have lovely neat corners. Notch each of the curves on the bone, too.

6 Carefully turn your bone the right way out through the gap you left. Stuff the bone with polyester stuffing/fibrefill.

7 Close the gap with ladder stitch. (See Step 6 on page 31, if you need to remind yourself how to do this.)

TO CLIP OR NOTCH?

As a rule of thumb, clip the fabric wherever you have a drastic change of direction in your sewing. You normally notch a convex curve (think of a hill) and clip into a concave curve or point (a valley). The reason behind this is that whatever you have done on the wrong side of the fabric – the side you usually work on – will be inverted, once it is turned out the right way. So, your bone-end curves that are sticking out face in the opposite direction when you are finished. If you don't clip or notch, you will see that they need to be done when you turn the project the right way out. This isn't too troublesome to rectify: it is a matter of just turning the project inside out again and fixing the problem.

TIP

You can buy the squeakers that go into these toys too!

TIP

Since this toy might take a bit of a beating, use small stitches to close the turning gap. If you're a little worried still, consider a machine stitch. This will be more visible, but will give that extra security.

Whew – all that clipping and notching was quite heavy and technical! In time, like everything else, you will know what to do at a glance.

Rope Bowl

By now, you have a bit of an idea about some of the more usual fabrics available to sewists of homewares. Of course, there are lots of stretchy ones and synthetics but they would fill several books on their own and are more the province of dressmakers. Let's just say that for sewing homewares, we have covered the popular choices.

But there is one material left that I wanted to talk to you about and it is quite a weird one… the clothesline rope. That's right; it's not a misprint. Your common, garden-variety cotton clothesline rope can be used to make a variety of items that you can sew on your home sewing machine. Rope makes are great to sew too, as you can create coasters, trivets, place mats and – for this project – bowls, and they all start the same way; you just stop sewing when they are big enough. I've chosen a bowl for this section as these rope makes are pretty satisfying to sew – literally, you can watch your project grow!

WHAT YOU WILL LEARN:

- About cotton rope
- Zigzag stitch
- Using fabric scraps

SEWING 101

About cotton rope

Simply head to your local hardware store to find some. Craft shops sell rope for the purpose of making baskets and similar, but it will cost more. For the best results, choose natural fibres; I have used cotton here, but hessian/burlap/jute or hemp are lovely alternatives to choose from.

Now, to be kind and not put your machine under too much stress, I would say that a 5mm (¼in) thick rope is the best choice. As luck would have it, that is the size most often sold. Saying that, this is a project which will pretty much kill your needle. It'll make it blunt and difficult to sew with afterwards, so this is a nice one to do when your needle has worked hard on lots of sewing projects and is nearing the end of its life. Keep a little collection of these old machine needles for this sort of purpose. Afterwards, you can throw them away knowing that you got every drop of goodness out.

So what stitch do we need to use? We will explore a new one we haven't played with yet – zigzag stitch. You will find it in one form or another on all modern machines. The zigzag you select has to be wide enough to breach the gap between the two pieces of rope. It must go from halfway on one piece of rope to halfway on the next one to it, so that it will hold the two lengths together securely.

Using fabric scraps

By now, if you have been making along with me, you will have made a few things and accumulated a nice scrap collection. If there is a law in sewing, it is never throw anything away! This project is one example of why: you can use the strips to wrap the rope as you sew, either to join up multiple short lengths of rope (so don't panic if you don't cut your clothesline long enough!) or to give your item a little bit of colour. In fact, it is your choice to wrap the whole thing, or just here and there for another effect. Have a sort through your scraps and see which ones match well together – this will make your bowl look more harmonious.

A leather finish

As I have mentioned in passing (well, OK, laboured the point incessantly), I love little leather details! This time, your leather scrap is serving more of a functional purpose. Once your bowl is complete, you'll find you're left with a 'hanging' end. In the pattern, I will show you how to cover this end with a simple, punched leather tab that looks lovely and makes your bowl look organically artisan. (That's a thing, I promise.)

A DIFFERENT ENDING

If you'd prefer to finish off your rope end another way, there are two alternatives you could use. Wrapping the ends with more glued scraps of fabric is an effective, decorative way to finish them and prevents the ends from fraying (it uses up those extra fabric scraps too!); or, you can wrap the end with perle coton à broder.

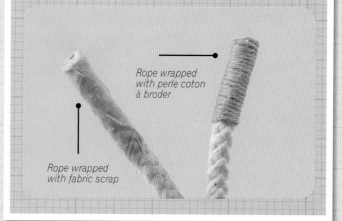

Rope wrapped with perle coton à broder

Rope wrapped with fabric scrap

PATTERN

Here's all there is to making these lovely bowls, which crop up on social media from time to time. The main thing is to go slow and think of your machine. If it is labouring (listen to the motor), STOP and see what the problem is. Other than that, these are very easy to make.

GATHER THESE SUPPLIES:

- ◉ Fabric
  - 10–15m (11–16½yd) length of cotton rope
  - Twelve scraps of fabric, cut into long strips approx. 3–4cm (1¼–1½in) long
  - Scrap of leather, cut into a 2.5 x 5cm (1 x 2in) strip
- ◉ Strong embroidery thread: I have used green perle coton à broder
- ◉ Awl (or see 'Optional')
- ◉ Extra strong, all-purpose crafting glue
- ◉ Your essential sewing kit (see page 11)
- ◉ Optional: revolving leather-punch pliers

1 Begin by gluing the end of the rope to stop it from fraying, and leave it to dry.

2 Now hold the glued end and fold the next bit of rope very close to it. Carefully wrap the rope around this fold to begin making a coil.

3 Holding the coil securely between your fingers, start sewing a zigzag stitch over the gaps in between the rope to hold the spiral together. Keep sewing steadily, rolling the rope around the initial coil until you have a coaster-sized circle (about 10–12 wraps).

TIP

You may need to adjust the stitch length of your zigzag stitch to make it bridge the gaps between the coils. If you're not sure how to do this, check your sewing machine manual, as each machine will have its own way of setting this up.

TIP

You could stop here with a coaster if you wish! Simply make more in the same way to have a nice set. Or if you keep coiling and sewing flat even further, eventually you'll end up with a nice placemat – or trivet, or pot-plant mat (it really is up to you).

THAT'S A WRAP

Start including the wraps of fabric, if you wish. (You can leave the coiled rope under the sewing machine needle for a moment while you do this.) Take a strip and put a dab of glue at one end. Start wrapping it around the rope at an angle to cover it – wrapping it straight won't work because it is less secure, and you want the fabric strip to to travel along the rope. When the wrap is almost complete, glue it at the other end too. Then, just pretend that it isn't there and keep sewing as before. Sew a bit further and then repeat. Continue to do this throughout.

TIP

You could also wrap perle coton à broder around your rope, or even use leftover bits of bias tape, for this stage too. Just make sure they are long enough so that they are easy to handle.

TIP

Think about what you will use your bowl for, as this can affect your choice of material. A cotton rope is easier to sew and kinder on the needle, but hessian/burlap/jute and hemp can produce higher, firmer sides as they are much stiffer – ideal for a bowl that will hold heavier items.

4 Start to tilt the sewn rope a little under the machine needle as you coil and stitch. You'll see a curved edge start to form. Increase the height gradually and smoothly, or lift the coil straight up once you have made a full-tilted circle on your machine. Now, all you have to do is to decide how high you want the sides to be. For the average fruit basket, the sides are about 8–10cm (3¼–4in) high, but there are no rules here and you can experiment.

5 To finish, cut and glue the end of your rope in the same way as you did at the beginning. Oversew the end, taking the needle through it to the coil underneath to secure it in place. With an awl (or revolving leather-punch pliers), punch two holes at each end of the leather strip. Glue the leather over the stitched end of the rope, and then use the perle coton à broder to sew it in place through the holes.

LINGO: 'OVERSEW'
To sew with stitches passing over an edge to make a very firm seam.

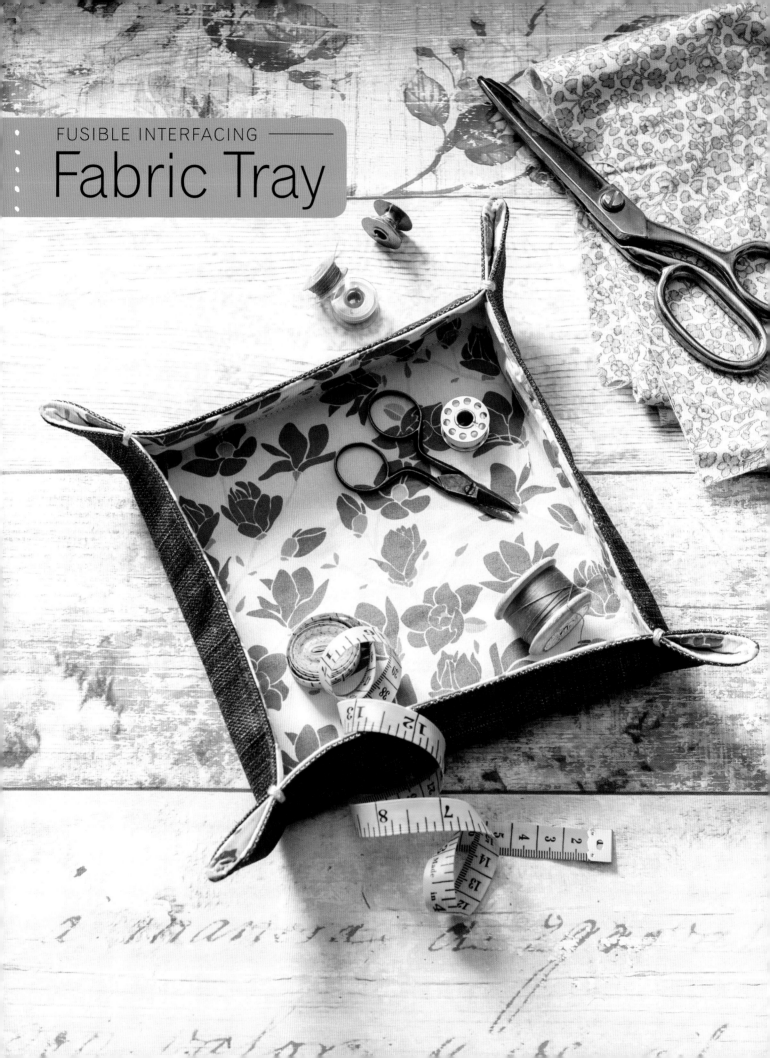

Fabric Tray

It's all about the fabric, right? That is what you see after all… Well, no. Actually not at all. Once you see your sewing with proper interfacing in, you will never go back.

After reading about the different types of interfacing in the materials section (see page 9), you may have been thinking it all sounds horribly confusing. It certainly is for a beginner, and I acknowledge your frustration because I have been there myself. So, let's break it down and have a look at the first of the six main interfacing types I'll be covering in this book (the easiest one too), and you will see that it isn't actually too bad.

(see page 9)

SEWING 101

About the first fusible interfacing

For our first project, we'll be using a light, non-woven, fusible wadding/batting, such as H630 by Vlieseline®. Yep, that's its name, and it's not a chemical formula! It is so useful that if you ever see it on special offer, buy it in quantity; I guarantee that it will change your sewing. You can usually buy it in lengths off a roll, and a metre (39in) will give you quite a lot to play with.

I love it because it adds just a little bit of padding, perfect especially on whisper-light fabrics like the lovely Pima cottons that I have used in this book.

However, I also like to use it on heavy denim as it adds a certain plumpness to the fabric; when you stitch into it, the stitches obligingly bury themselves into the fabric and look so professional. In addition, it is wonderful for bag making and perfect for layering over stronger, more structural interfacings (but more on that later…)

We are going to use this thin wadding/batting to make a fabric tray this time, and it is ever-so-slight padded, which will give our make just enough oomph and structure. We will be cutting the interfacing to the same size as our fabric piece too, which is unusual for most sewing projects. Remember how we cut fabric in the corner to reduce bulk? Interfacing is the same: most of the time, you cut the interfacing so it is slightly smaller, so that it isn't in the seam allowance when you sew. Here, we don't need to worry about that, so don't fuss around trying to make your interfacing smaller: this type isn't that bulky, and we actually need to add structure to the seams too.

When I am working with fusible interfacing, I like to work in a well-ventilated area; I also have a cloth handy to place over what I am interfacing, so that the glue side (which will be facing up as we iron it to the fabric sitting on top of it) doesn't find itself stuck to my iron plate. Keep checking as you iron on the interfacing too, to see if it has fused successfully. Some fabrics are easier to fuse interfacing onto than others, and some will take a little extra time.

ALL WADDING/BATTING IS INTERFACING, BUT NOT ALL INTERFACING IS WADDING/ BATTING

Interfacing is a general term which refers to the support structures inserted invisibly between fabrics to do a very specific job. Some are soft and pliable, like quilt wadding/batting, and some are really stiff – like corset supports. So wadding/batting can be said to be an interfacing because it has a job to do between the fabric layers, but no stretch of the imagination could call the material that keeps a baseball cap peak stiff a 'wadding/batting'.

LINGO:
'WADDING' OR 'BATTING'

Some sewists use wadding, others use batting, so what is the difference? Nothing! In the UK you will mostly hear it called 'wadding', while in the US it is known as 'batting'.

PATTERN

Right, this interfacing is so simple to use that we don't need to go into it any further. Let's move on to the project! These trays are so useful. You will find uses for them all over the house.

1 Begin by cutting a 25cm (10in) square from each fabric.

2 Lay the interfacing onto the wrong side of the lining fabric and iron until the heat of the iron melts the glue and bonds the interfacing to the fabric (fuses).

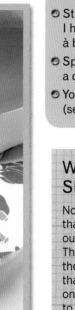

GATHER THESE SUPPLIES:

⚬ Fabric
  - FQ of pretty floral quilting cotton, for the lining
  - FQ of coordinating quilting cotton, for the tray outer
⚬ Interfacing
  - 25cm (10in) square of light-weight, non-woven, fusible wadding/batting: I have used H630 by Vlieseline®
⚬ Strong embroidery thread: I have used pink perle coton à broder
⚬ Spray bottle filled with water plus a cotton bud/swab
⚬ Your essential sewing kit (see page 11)

WHICH FABRIC SHOULD I INTERFACE?

Normally, you interface the fabric that is destined to be seen on the outside of a project, like a bag outer. This tray is a bit confusing because the lining is actually more visible than the 'proper' outside fabric. So, on this occasion, fuse the interfacing to the wrong side of the lining.

3 Pin the interfaced lining fabric to the non-interfaced coordinating fabric, the right sides together, and sew all the way around the edge, leaving a small turning gap in one side. Clip across the corners to reduce bulk, then turn the tray the right way out through the gap.

4 Press so that the edges are perfect and then top-stitch very narrowly right around the outer edge. This will close the turning gap at the same time.

5 Measure in 4cm (1½in) from one corner, on each side, and draw a line from one end to the other for each side, using a water-soluble pen. Repeat in the other corner. You should have marked a square right around the tray, as shown.

6 Top-stitch along the lines of the central square only. This will make the folding lines, which you'll raise later to give your tray a nice, lifted edge. When the stitching is done, remove as much of the marker lines as you can by spraying the fabric with cold water and rubbing the lines away with a cotton bud/swab.

HOW THICK SHOULD MY INTERFACING BE?

As a rule of thumb, choose an interfacing about the same weight as your fabric, or a touch lighter – if the interfacing is heaver than the fabric, the item (or garment, if you're dressmaking) will sit or hang oddly. So, the heavier the fabric, the heavier the interfacing.

TIP

Although interfacings are not free, they go a long way, so don't panic at the prospect of buying a stash every time you buy fabric. There are some tricks to joining interfacing too, which you'll see later in the book (see page 89), so never think there will be wastage and don't throw out the offcuts!

7 On one side of the tray, fold the tray towards the lining, along the folding line. Press to create a nice crease. Repeat on each side. Pinch one corner together (they will cooperate because of the second top-stitch line) and oversew the perle coton à broder at the marked top edges to anchor them in place. Repeat for the other three corners.

Pot-Plant Bag

So. We've entered the dark world of interfacings. I've been trying to convince you that interfacing is indispensable. If the tray hasn't cut it, I thought we'd sew something that really shows you its benefits.

In addition to interfacing, this make will give you a chance to learn a couple more skills which I know you will love. One of which is how to box a base (yep – there is some weird terminology in sewing!), and how to put a bag together. In fact, just in this little pot-plant holder, you will have two essential skills that are used in just about any bag pattern on the market!

Teehee – I see that I have your attention now.

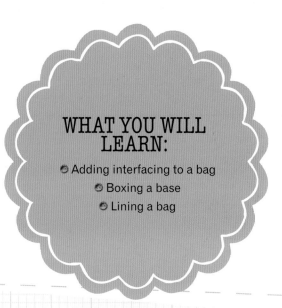

WHAT YOU WILL LEARN:

◎ Adding interfacing to a bag
◎ Boxing a base
◎ Lining a bag

SEWING 101

Boxing a base

What is boxing a base? Basically, it is about giving a base to something and, most importantly, adding to the volume and the shape of that something. So, instead of having a flat, 2D-like structure to your make, all of a sudden your item is more 3D, has depth and you can fit more things inside. Box bases are used a lot in bag making, so if that is where your aspirations lie this will be an invaluable skill to learn.

Best of all, the boxed-base technique is super easy to do. If you can manage falling off a log without help, you can nail this!

THE IMPORTANCE OF INTERFACING

Before negotiating the actual pattern, I thought it would be interesting to show you how important a part interfacing plays in something like a bag. Here is what our make looks like with and without interfacing. See how the one on the right has some soft structure and sits nicely? Now look at the sad sack (literally) on the left. Enough said. Sometimes a picture really is worth a thousand words.

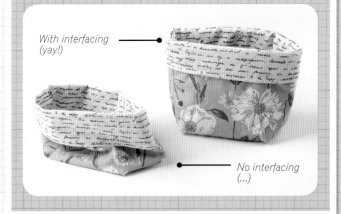

With interfacing (yay!)

No interfacing (...)

Lining a bag

When you put a bag together, you don't want raw seams. Anywhere. Period. Even if they are very neatly overlocked or zigzagged, they look awful and will make your work look amateurish. Besides which, they are not necessary. As sewists, we have all sorts of tricks to bury them and the technique I will show you in detail soon is the daddy of them all! This is where that turning gap from earlier becomes your best friend. So what's the technique? Well, we're going to line our bag.

Leaving a turning gap in your lining is very important, and the reason why will become apparent when we look at putting the bag together in a moment (see page 47). Now, as a general rule, the turning gap goes on the bottom seam but it cannot get in the way of the boxed corners (this will make a little more sense in a moment). So, when you think about how big the gap has to be, make it only just large enough to do the job and take care it doesn't get too close to your bottom corners.

Especially for bag making, whatever you do to the outer you will do to the lining too, so that it fits snugly together. In fact, I would advise you to have a go at boxing the base of your lining first, before you stitch the outer bag. That way, not only can you hide any initial wonkiness inside the make (if there is any), but it is less work if it has to be replaced altogether because there is no interfacing in the lining.

LINGO: 'OVERLOCKED'

This a general word describing a whole series of special stitches made on an **overlocker**, a sister of our regular machine. Sometimes known as a **serger**, this machine is specially made to finish seams or edges of fabric neatly and professionally – mostly through special stitches (some machines can trim the fabric in a certain way, too, to stop it from fraying along the edges). Overlockers tend to be used for dressmaking, especially for finishing trickier-to-sew fabrics like georgette and knit; so, if you go down that route, it may be worth investing in one.

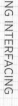

PATTERN

Pot-plant bags are lovely to have around the home to house your urban jungle – especially if the pots your plants come with are not actually that nice. This make is quick to sew too, and we can't complain about that...

GATHER THESE SUPPLIES:

- Fabric
  - FQ of pretty floral quilting cotton, for the outer
  - FQ of contrasting quilting cotton, for the lining
- Interfacing
  - Two 25cm (10in) squares of light, non-woven, fusible wadding/batting: I have used H630 by Vlieseline®
- Your essential sewing kit (see page 11)

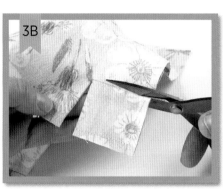

1 From the outer and lining fabrics, cut two 23cm (9in) square pieces each. Fuse the squares of interfacing to the wrong side of each outer fabric piece. Trim the interfacing to the size of the outer squares.

2 Pin the two outer fabric squares right sides together and sew along three sides only. Pin the lining pieces right sides together and sew three sides as before but, this time, leave a turning gap in the centre of the bottom seam.

3 Time to box the base. Don't worry; it's easy. You will need to cut a square from the two bottom corners. This is a bit scary because, well, cutting! Let's go one step at a time. For the purposes of demonstration, I have left out the interfacing so you can see what I am doing. Measure and mark a 4cm (1½in) square on the bottom two corners of both the lining and the outer [A]. When you're happy with your drawn squares, cut them out [B].

4 Now pinch the seams together [A]. This means bringing the bottom seam up so that it meets and matches the side seam – this is to make the seaming neater. The two bag panels will stick out at the sides. Press the seams flat and pin them in place, then sew across them using a normal seam allowance [B]. Repeat this process exactly with the seams on the other side, and for the joined lining panels (or the outer, if you practised on the lining). You have box based both pieces!

TIP

You may notice that the stitches come undone at the square corners a bit because you have just cut them. I tend to shorten my stitch length as I approach the corner to be cut out (and you will know this corner will be cut, because you read the pattern right through before beginning, remember?...). Shortening the stitch length packs more stitches in, and means that they are less likely to come undone.

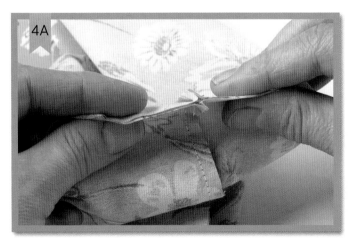

5 Now for the sewist trick. Make sure that your outer is the right way out (the nice sides facing outwards). The lining should be already inside out. Now pull the lining on over the outer and match up the side seams perfectly.

6 Pin all around the top edge – I like to pin the side seams first, as shown. Now sew that top edge all the way around, leaving no gaps. Remove the pins.

7 Now turn the whole bag out through that gap that you left in the lining, being careful not to stretch the stitches (or worse, tear them) then close the gap by machine with top-stitching.

8 Now stuff the lining down into the bag and press that top seam so that it is perfect. Top-stitch narrowly around the edge (this helps to keep the lining down).

9 Turn the cuff of the bag over by about 5cm (2in). Do have a bit of a play here – it is up to you how far you'd like to turn them to make the bag fit the pot.

TIP

You might need to reduce the bulk on the outer side seams by plucking the interfacing away a bit. You rarely need to do this, but it's a quick way of conquering that extra bit of thickness that will stress the seams, and it won't disrupt the rest of your make.

Now you have two of the skills central to making the most complicated of bags! They come under the heading of It's Easy When You Know How.

I am hoping that the 'with' and 'without' photos from last time (see page 45) convinced you that interfacing is really important. As you continue through this book, and make more complicated projects, you will see it for yourself again and again. It seems odd that something that we never see is so vital, but let me put it this way: does your house have foundations? Do you see them? Case closed!

I have a new interfacing for you this time, and I want to show you another tricky piece of sorcery – layering interfacing.

WHAT YOU WILL LEARN:

◉ About the next fusible interfacing
◉ Layering interfacing
◉ Introducing snap fasteners
◉ Bagging out

SEWING 101

About the next fusible interfacing

The next type of interfacing is is thin, non-woven and fusible (like the H630) but is designed to have a little more rigidity, adding a bit more structure to a make – great for bags and collars. The thin structuring instantly makes your project more professional, as it adds a crispness to the look and feel. The type I use is called 'Decovil I Light' (I know right, who names these?). Decovil I Light has a big brother too, simply called 'Decovil', and between the two of them they add great, gentle support. Sort of like a favourite friend. For this reason, I especially love using the Decovil brothers for bag flaps.

I actually use Decovil I Light more than its older sibling because that little bit of structure is all that is needed; however, I rarely use it on its own. It is great individually on something like denim, which is a thicker material, but if you have a beautiful fine cotton like the ones that we are using here, it will feel too papery and bubbles may form when you fuse it on. Fusible interfacings can do that sometimes and the result is ugly. Here's where the layering comes in.

Layering interfacing

I love to stack thin, fusible interlining on a slightly thicker wadding/batting, like H630. The result? A firm, cushioned support and no bubble danger. These layers are also super easy to top-stitch or sew and the results will speak for themselves. To make your layers, fuse the wadding/batting first (this gives the fabric a billowy softness) then lay the Decovil I on top of it – simply iron this onto the wadding/batting.

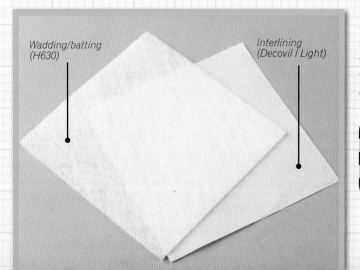

Wadding/batting (H630)

Interlining (Decovil I Light)

Introducing snap fasteners

It is time to introduce a new item and a new toy to go with it – snap fasteners! These plastic closures are easy to install and they look really nice – especially as you can buy them in all sorts of colours, making coordinating them with your fabrics very easy (and fun!) too.

Snap fasteners are often used for children's clothes (those of you who have had small children will remember seeing them all too often when nappy changing) but these guys are also good for closing openings on bags and homewares as well.

To insert them, you will need to buy a nifty setting tool (which, for some reason, proudly boasts that it is made from bullet-proof steel! I am not sure if it is going to get a lot of that sort of action in a sewing room), but this isn't expensive to buy. The snap fasteners themselves are not an expensive piece of kit to pop in your sewing box either. You can buy them in mixed packs, and as a beginner I recommend starting with a size 20 as this is the average size. They do come in other sizes (and shapes, too, like hearts and flowers) but then you need to buy other attachments and tools. Start with one size and tool, and I promise you that you will use them a lot.

So how do we use these snaps? There are two halves of every snap and (politically correct activists please look away now) they are commonly known as a male half and a female half. You position the male half of the snap on the flap of a purse or wallet and the female half on the other part of the make (often a pocket or inside the bag along the back); this means the male half can go into the female (I promise that I didn't make this up; you should see some of the terms that plumbers use!) and close the opening effectively.

Each of the halves comes in a further two halves (this is harder to explain than to master, so bear with me). Each of the halves' halves goes on either side of the fabric of your make and then the special nifty tool (known as snap pliers) splays the post on the snap so that it stays there. The same goes for the other piece, and the other pair of halves.

> ### LINGO: 'INTERLINING'
> **Interlining** is a layer between the fabric and lining. It could be anything, from another layer of fabric to wadding/batting or felt.

PATTERN

Well, that leaves us with the pattern! This time it is a loyalty-card wallet, and a really handy thing to have in your bag to keep all those extra cards together.

1 Using the template on Pattern Sheet B, cut out three pieces – one from the outer fabric, and one from each interfacing. Fuse the H630 onto the wrong side of the floral fabric, and then iron the Decovil I Light over the top.

2 Roughly cut a piece of lining fabric from your F8th, measuring 14 x 24cm (5½ x 9½in). Don't trim it yet.

3 With the right sides together, sew the lining to the interfaced outer, leaving a small gap on one side for turning out. Trim the lining back to the same size and shape as the outer.

4 Clip the corners, notch the curve and turn out through the gap, being very careful to poke out the corners gently with your trusty chopstick to make them nice and sharp.

5 Press the wallet, folding the edges of the gap inside at the same time. Ladder stitch the gap closed. (See page 31, Step 6 if you need reminding how to do this.) Top-stitch the short, straight edge only, using a narrow seam allowance. This will become the top front edge of the wallet when it is folded up.

6 There are two lines on the template to show you where to fold the wallet. Find them, and then transfer them to the fabric with a water-soluble marker pen. Fold the fabric along these lines and then pin the fold in place. Top-stitch the wallet, beginning at the bottom of the left-hand side, sewing clockwise all the way around the flap, then stitching down the other side.

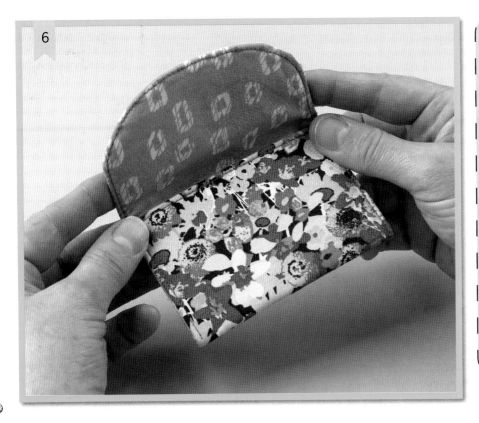

GATHER THESE SUPPLIES:

- ◎ Fabric
  - F8th of floral quilting cotton, for the outer
  - F8th of contrasting quilting cotton, for the lining
- ◎ Interfacing
  - 15 x 25cm (6 x 10in) piece of light-weight, non-woven, fusible wadding/batting: I have used H630 by Vlieseline®
  - 15 x 25cm (6 x 10in) piece of light-weight, non-woven, fusible interlining: I have used Decovil I Light by Vlieseline®
- ◎ Awl (or see 'Optional')
- ◎ Snap fastener set plus snap pliers: I have used KAM snaps in size 20
- ◎ Your essential sewing kit (see page 11)
- ◎ Optional: revolving leather-punch pliers

TEMPLATE ON PATTERN SHEET B

LINGO: 'BAGGING OUT'

Bagging out is a technique used in most sewing designs. The best way to define it is that it is sewing your project inside out, with all the right sides together initially, and then turning the make the right way out through a gap you have left deliberately, so that all the ugly bits are hidden inside.

Sound familiar? That's because you have already done it every time you have made something from this book that started with the pieces right sides together! 'Bagging out' is the proper name for the technique.

So why mention it now? Because it is another piece of technical language that will make reading sewing patterns easier. It is always worth learning the language of what you are doing, to help deepen your understanding in the long run.

7 Now to attach the snap fasteners. To begin with, you need a hole. Using the template and a water-soluble marker pen, draw a cross onto the fabric flap where the template indicates, and a corresponding one on the straight section of the wallet for the female half (see tip, right). With an awl (or revolving leather-punch pliers), punch a hole through the cross.

8 Take the male halves of the snap and place them together, through the flap hole, with the fabric in between them.

9 Nestle the flat cap part in the bottom of the snap pliers and line everything up. Squeeze. Done!

10 Do the same with the female halves. This time, the rounded cap goes on the inside of the wallet. Get it all lined up and squeeze again. Your snap is on!

TIP

You'll need to work out where to place the female half yourself. Don't panic! It is really simple to do. All you have to do is to put the first snap on and then fold the wallet flap down and make a mark directly onto the fabric where the female half is to go.

TIP

Do check the placement of your snaps because although they are not impossible to get off, it is really hard; you will likely need to break the snap fastener with pliers to remove it, and in turn the effort could wreck your project. Always have a practice if you are a bit nervous. They are cheap, and once you understand how they work you can use them everywhere.

Well, this is getting exciting now! You have so many concepts under your belt now, that I feel confident about introducing something which feels a bit more advanced (but really isn't).

This make is a pair of slippers, and we have a few things to introduce before getting down to the real business.

WHAT YOU WILL LEARN:

◉ Sew-in interfacing
◉ Making something you can wear (sewing 3D shapes)
◉ Dabbling with quilting
◉ Adding bias binding

SEWING 101

Sew-in interfacing

It was going to happen, folks. You've got away with happily fusing your interfacing onto your fabric, but now we're taking a step further and sewing in our interfacing.

Sew-in is used here, mainly because the brand that I love the most has this only as a sew-in! However, even if it was available in fusible, these slippers are better off with sew-in because you are quilting as you go, and fusible interfacing doesn't work well with this technique. Sew-in interfacings are also used in bag making; this is because they are stronger and more reliable, especially after washing the product. That is not an issue here because the interfacing is very securely sewn down but, sometimes, fusibles can come loose and shift away from the seams, causing unsightly bunching.

There are three types of interfacing we'll be using for these slippers, one for the upper and two for the sole. The first of our sew-ins, used for the upper, is my favourite interfacing and is a low-loft wadding/batting often used in quilting. The type I use is called (enigmatically) #279 80/20 cotton mix wadding/batting. We need to speak to the people about these names! It is actually a bit difficult to buy small amounts of this type of interfacing because it is designed for quilting, and quilters rarely make tiny quilts. What most sewists do is to save the offcuts from a larger project. But, as we are starting from scratch here, take some time to shop around and see how small a piece you can get for yourself. Aim for about a 30cm (12in) strip (most places will not sell less than 25cm (10in) strips).

For the soles of the slippers, we're going to layer interfacing again. One layer is a light-weight, non-woven, fusible wadding/batting, such as H630 (see, we're not leaving him too quickly...), and the other is a light-weight, sew-in foam interfacing. This provides a nice layer of cushioning, keeps its own shape and gives gentle structure too. I like to use Style-Vil by Vlieseline®. The only thing that we need to remember for a make with this type of interfacing (and other projects that include it) is that there is a trade-off. Yes, it is like walking on a cloud, but it cannot

deliver a smooth, padded surface if there is too much bulk in the seams. The way to combat this is, once the interfacing is sewn to the main fabric, to trim it smaller all around, right back to the seam line. This keeps the interfacing in place securely but takes just enough of the interfacing out of the seam, removing bulk and giving your sewing machine a bit of a break.

Now as Style-Vil is a sew-in interfacing, I encourage you to machine sew it on as detailed above because this makes it much more secure and less likely to move around on the base of your slipper. Just ensure you take a small, very sharp pair of scissors to snip the interfacing right back to the seam line – smaller scissors will allow you to get as close to the seam as possible. However, if you are a little nervous about trimming back to the seam, there is an alternative: extra-strong crafting glue! If you choose this option, ensure you trim back the Style-Vil sole by 5mm (¼in) all around and centre it well over the fabric sole, before gluing it into place.

Making something you can wear (sewing 3D shapes)

The first thing that people worry about when making clothing of any sort is the fit. I don't normally make things to fit humans for this very reason, but slippers are an exception because they are somehow so satisfying.

I have provided a basic size option, but what happens if you (or the intended recipient's feet) need some extra size tweaking? Well, the good news is that slippers are a relaxed fit so they are not a super tailored item. This gives you a bit of wiggle room (quite literally), especially in terms of width. My advice to you is to stand on the pattern template in bare feet or socks and see if you need to add more or less to the outline. As I said, slippers are satisfying because they are a bit forgiving.

These slippers require you to cut and sew the fabric in a certain way, in order to create and hold a shape. This is known as 3D sewing. This sort of sewing often worries people but, to be honest, 3D is not much harder than what you've done already. Again, a good pattern will tell you what to do; some even include pattern markings too, and all you need to do is to match them up. With our slippers, which are a beginner's pattern (yes really!), the important part is to find the middle of the sole on the toe part, as this will help you place the upper in the correct place – and this is marked on the template. See? Easy.

Dabbling with quilting

Another term is going to be bandied about in this chapter: QAYQ.

Um. What?

QAYG stands for 'Quilt As You Go', and it is the most fun that you can have with a scrap basket! If you have been sewing along (and I hope that you have) you will have generated scraps and offcuts and NO WAY do these belong in the bin! Always keep them as we can make things like this.

Quilting will be properly dealt with in the 'Quilting & Patching' chapter on pages 78–99, but I wanted to do a little sneak peek here. Normally, as you will see later, quilting and patching are two separate activities. With QAYG, it is all done at once! And it is perfect for a make like our slippers.

Adding bias binding

To neaten the edges of your slipper shapes, and create a professional finish, we're going to add **bias binding**. I will go into more detail on binding as we encounter other methods later on but let's start with a quick overview here.

There are two sorts of binding – straight and bias. Straight binding is cut on the straight grain (up and down or across) and bias binding is cut on the diagonal or bias grain of fabric. This means that bias binding is a bit stretchy and you can mould it around a curve. Don't even think about using straight binding for a project like this! It has to be bias or it will pucker in the most ugly way on the curves.

We're using bought bias binding for this make, but for now it's useful to understand how it works and why. It is a pet hate of mine to see a wonderful project let down because someone tried to use straight binding to negotiate a curve.

PATTERN

Using a combination of stylish fabrics, leather, corresponding bias binding and cushiony interfacing, let's make a pair of slippers that feel ultra-luxe!

1 Using the template on Pattern Sheet B, begin by cutting two mirror-image sole pieces from the FQ of contrasting fabric. Fuse the H630 to the wrong sides of each one, then trim back the interfacing on each sole so that they are the same size and shape as the contrasting fabric sole.

TIP

You must cut out your soles mirror image, and there are two ways to achieve this. Either fold the fabric in half and cut the two out at the same time (and they will 'magically' be mirror image), or – in the case of the thicker leather later – cut one out, flip the template over to the other side and then cut out the other.

2 Using the template again, cut out two mirror-image pieces from Style-Vil. Then, you can either centre the Style-Vil shapes over their respective interfaced fabric soles as much as you can – over the H360, sew them in place and then trim back the Style-Vil to the seam; or, you can trim the soles by 5mm (¼in) all around, so that they are smaller than the interfaced fabric soles, centre them over the soles and then glue them on top of the H360. (See also the explanation on page 53).

GATHER THESE SUPPLIES:

- Fabric
  - Scraps of pretty quilting cotton, for the slipper upper
  - FQ of contrasting quilting cotton, for the lining and for backing the soles
  - F8th of leather, for the soles
- Interfacing
  - 25cm (10in) square of flexible, light-weight, sew-in foam wadding/batting: I have used Style-Vil by Vlieseline®
  - 25cm (10in) square of light-weight, non-woven, fusible wadding/batting: I have used H630 by Vlieseline®
  - 25cm (10in) square of soft, light-weight, cotton/polyester mix, sew-in wadding/batting: I have used #279 80/20 cotton mix by Vlieseline®
- 2.5m (2¾yd) length of bias binding
- Extra strong, all-purpose crafting glue
- Your essential sewing kit (see page 11)
- Optional: small length of decorative ribbon – I have used one with a Union Jack print

TEMPLATES ON PATTERN SHEET B

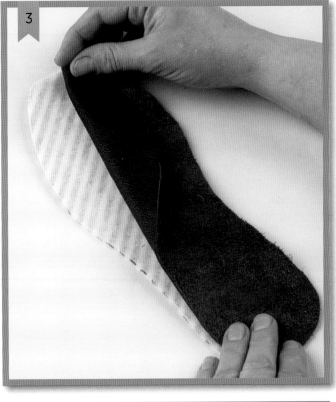

3 If you have glued on the Style-Vil sole, wait until it has dried before continuing.

Taking your sole template once more, cut out two mirror-image pieces from leather. Place one interfaced sole in front of you, the right sides of the fabric facing down, then glue on a corresponding leather sole on top, suede side facing up. The soles are ready to use.

IMPORTANT NOTE: To show some of the layers you need, I am demonstrating this stage without the Style-Vil glued on. However, please ensure the Style-Vil layer is sewed or glued on, over the H360, before applying the leather sole.

4 Make the uppers next. Allowing yourself plenty of working room, use the upper template on Pattern Sheet B to draw the uppers onto the #279 wadding/batting with a water-soluble marker pen.

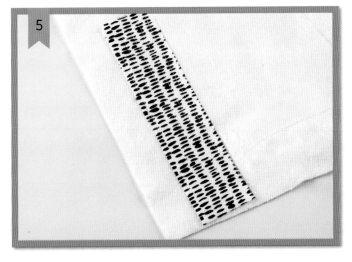

5 Now for that QAYG method. Choose a scrap and cut it into a rectangle or square: mine is 10 x 4cm (4 x 1½in). The idea is to 'colour in' your drawn shape with fabric. Lay the strip onto one wadding/batting upper on the far left- or right-hand side of the outline, over the lines and sew it in place. To do this, simply sew lines from top to bottom across the whole shape (this is the quilting bit), about 1cm (⅜in) apart. This creates a pattern on your shape and secures it in place. Going over the outline of the slipper upper is really important, to ensure the whole upper is coloured in with scraps. You will need to redraw the outline later, once all the scraps are sewn on, to help you cut out the upper.

> **TIP**
>
> The scraps do not have to have the same arrangement on both slippers. As long as the colours correspond and the fabrics coordinate, they will work well as a pair. The pattern can be entirely random.

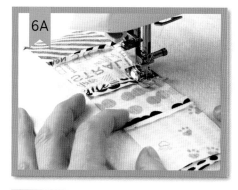

6A

6B

6C

6 Pick another scrap shape – I have some rough squares measuring 4 x 5cm (1½ x 2in) which I have sewn right sides together, then pressed the seams flat, so that they equal roughly the length of the first strip. Lay this next scrap shape on top of the first strip, right sides together, and then sew a seam along the right-hand side (or left-hand side, if you're working from right to left) [**A**]. Now, flip it over and finger press the seam – I have used a seam roller for ease [**B**]. Quilt lines as you did before, in Step 5 [**C**].

SEAM PRESSING FOR QUILTING

Did you know that you don't always have to press with an iron? It pleases Fitbits® to run back and forth to the iron but, sometimes, all that is necessary is to finger press. This means running your finger along the edge of the piece to be creased. If you want a sharper crease, use your nail. You can buy various implements to do this, but to be honest fingers are more convenient. The only problem with finger pressing is that it can distort delicate bias cuts and pull them out of shape: as you are running your finger along the fabric, you are essentially dragging it and this can cause the fabric to ripple along the edge – even ruin it. So, keep finger pressing for straight-grain cuts.

7 Continue to lay the scraps onto your drawn upper in this way, using a mix of long and square scraps, until the whole shape is covered. Use the template of the upper to help your redraw the upper shape back in. Repeat Steps 5–7 for the other upper.

8 Lay the upper onto the untrimmed lining, wrong sides together, and pin.

LINING QAYG PROJECTS

Sometimes QAYG is done with the lining already included, but I don't like this method because you have no chance to hide the awful messy bits on the back. I prefer to quilt then introduce the lining afterwards.

8

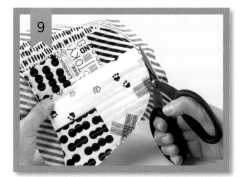

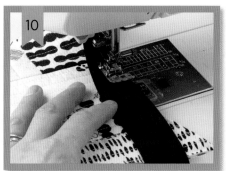

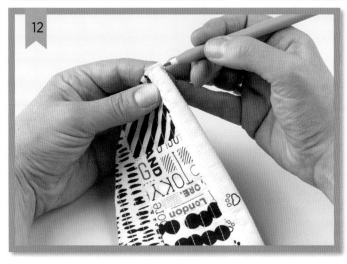

9 Sew all around the perimeter of one upper and then cut it out.

10 The next thing to do is to neaten that top edge. This is done with bias binding. So how do we put the binding on? Well my favourite method is half machine and half hand-sewn. To begin with, unfold your bought bias binding and lay one edge along the curve of one of your uppers, the folded side facing up. Sew along that lined-up edge with a normal 5mm (¼in) seam allowance.

11 Now fold the binding over the raw edge of the upper and over to the lining side to hide it, tucking the long creased edge inside. Pin the binding in place, then hand-sew this side on with ladder stitches. Repeat for the other upper piece.

12 Use the template to help you mark in the centre of the uppers. Alternatively, fold the uppers in half and mark the centre fold. Match up the marks on the uppers with the centre marks on the soles and pin them together.

13 Sew the uppers onto the soles, the quilted side facing up. Trim away some of the seam allowance on the uppers and soles and then bind the whole of the sole edge with bias binding in exactly the same way as you did before (see the tip and technique boxes, too, left). If you wish, glue a bit of decorative ribbon onto the soles to finish.

CREATING A NEAT BEGINNING AND END TO YOUR BINDING

To create a neat finish for your bias binding, leave the beginning of the bias binding unstitched by approx. 2.5cm (1in) and fold the short end over to the creased side by 1cm (⅜in). When you've sewn on almost all your bias binding, and you're back at the beginning, tuck the end bit inside the beginning end of the bias binding by approx. 5mm (¼in); trim off the extra. Wrap the beginning binding around the trimmed end and then continue to sew as before. This will secure the wrapped ends in place.

TIP

As the leather soles are very difficult to stitch into by hand, sew the bias binding onto the bottom leather side first by machine, then finish off the binding by hand on the top side. That way, you can stitch into fabric instead.

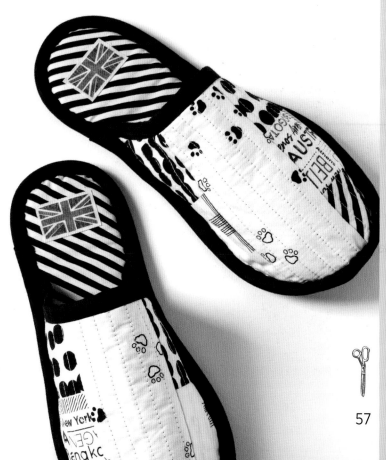

BEGINNER FME & EASY APPLIQUÉ
Cloud Pillow

In that last project you had plenty to do, and there were a few pretty involved techniques. So, well done if you stayed in the saddle. If you had a little trouble, keep practising. It really is worth it!

This time, we're working on an easier make and it's a lot of fun. The best bit is that we are now delving into the world of appliqué and embellishment, which will give your item a lot of character (literally).

SEWING 101

Introducing appliqué

Appliqué is not only a great technique, it's also another fabulous way of using up scraps of fabric – in fact, you tend to use only very small scraps for appliqué, so this is just further proof that nothing should ever be thrown away. In addition, you need only a few things for appliqué – thread in the right colour, fabric glue, an embroidery hoop and a darning foot for your machine.

What is a darning foot?

A darning foot sounds boring. Who darns? Actually, it is time they gave it a snazzier name because it is about more than just holes in things. It is the foot that we use for free-motion embroidery (FME). More about that in a moment.

If you haven't got a darning foot for your machine, it's time to go shopping! You can buy generic ones that tend to fit most sewing machine brands. For instructions on how to attach the foot, please refer to your sewing machine's manual.

Most darning feet tend to look like the one you see to the left. It is super useful, as its shape allows you to move your work around and make random patterns. The large hole in the middle of the foot is designed to help you see your stitching below.

Typical darning foot; used mostly for FME.

Introduction to free-motion embroidery (or FME)

Let's look at the machine. Under the needle, there are some 'teeth' – rows of rough squares or rectangles poking out of the needle plate. These are the 'feed dogs' and they help to pull your fabric through the machine as you sew. However, they only feed the fabric forwards or backwards through the machine. The trouble is that when we use the darning foot for FME, we also want to go to the left and right and around about. Well, the feed dogs will not allow that.

The answer is to drop them out of the way. Have a look at your manual for the specifics, but most modern machines have a way (usually a lever) that lets you do this. If you have an older sewing machine, set the stitch length to zero and this will disable them and allow you to do the same job.

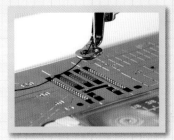
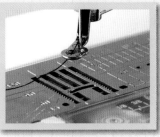

Feed dogs up (regular sewing).   *Feed dogs down (FME).*

With the feed dogs out of the way, we can now move the project around and write words, embroider things and go back and forth as much as we want to. The thing is, though, fabric is soft and bendy, and doesn't want to play nicely if we're sewing all over the place. We need an easy way of making this fabric stiffer and more rigid, to prevent the fabric puckering up as we stitch. The answer? An embroidery hoop. Your cheap, common, garden-variety hoop will hold the fabric taut and allow you to see what you're doing. The only difference in the way you use it is that you'll be sewing with the hoop upside down. Why? As the presser foot will want to hold the fabric against the needle plate, you still need to have the fabric as close to it as possible; if the hoop was the right way up, the fabric would be about 1cm (⅜in) too high.

Now we have everything that we need, let's tackle FME. **FME, or free-motion embroidery**, is pretty much what it says on the can. 'Free-motion' means that you are free to go in any direction. It is a great way to doodle onto fabric and it is also great for holding down appliqué.

We will cover more details on FME in other makes but for today, we are using FME to do a type of appliqué called raggy appliqué. Again, no hidden meanings there – this kind of appliqué means all you need to do is stitch your cut scraps of fabric in place, and then leave the edges alone. No finishing required. We'll be tackling this in more detail later too (see pages 70–73).

PATTERN

This is an especially nice make for a nursery: the two emotions expressed on the pillow are easy for children to understand and can make a nice communication and teaching tool, too. Sort of a 'how do you feel today?'.

GATHER THESE SUPPLIES:

◎ Fabric
  - FQ of bright quilting cotton, for the smiley front
  - FQ of patterned grey quilting cotton, for the sad back
  - Scraps of black solid, for the eyes (Note: please check the template to work out how much you need)
◎ Interfacing
  - 50 x 100cm (19¾ x 39½in) piece of light-weight, non-woven, fusible wadding/batting: I have used H630 by Vlieseline®
◎ Polyester stuffing/fibrefill
◎ Fabric acrylic paint in white
◎ Spray bottle filled with water and a cotton bud/swab
◎ Your essential sewing kit (see page 11), plus darning foot

TEMPLATES ON PATTERN SHEET A

1 Begin by fusing the H630 to the wrong side of both fabrics. Using the template on Pattern Sheet A, draw the cloud outline onto the right side of each fused fabric piece. Make sure one cloud shape is a mirror image of the other. Do not cut the clouds out yet.

2 Using the template, cut out the eyes from your scraps of black fabric. Position these onto each cloud face and then glue them with fabric glue to secure temporarily. Using the template as your guide, draw the features of each cloud onto their respective fabrics – the smiley face on the bright fabric, the sad face on the grey – with a water-soluble marker pen.

3 The eyes look a bit dead at the moment. That is because a highlight is needed to give them life! Dip a pencil or a chopstick into the white acrylic paint and make a small dot in the same place on both eyes. See what a difference it makes! Allow to dry thoroughly.

TRANSFERRING A DESIGN

With FME and detailed stitching it is a good idea to add drawn outlines beforehand to act as handy guides to follow as you stitch. There are all sorts of highly specialized ways to transfer patterns to fabric, like pricking the pattern to make holes that you then mark through with chalk; however, I find the simplest way to transfer is to tape the pattern to a window (for obvious reasons, this method won't work at night), then tape the fabric over the top of it. Now use the water-soluble marker pen to trace over what you see. The only con here is that this method works best on light-coloured fabric, and one that's very thin. Remember, you will have to put the interfacing on beforehand too, which will make the fabric opaque. If you are still having trouble seeing the pattern, photocopy it and then go over the main lines on the paper with a thick black marker so that they are easier to see.

4 Hoop up, with the right side of your fabric facing up and the embroidery hoop upside down. Set up your machine for free-motion embroidery (make sure to check your sewing machine manual as you do this, as every machine is different). Embroider the features onto each fabric piece with black thread – a smiley face on the bright cloud, a sad one on the grey cloud – going over the same lines again once or twice more, to make them darker and scribbly in style. When you've finished, trim the thread ends away. Remove as much of the marker as you can by spraying the fabric with cold water and rubbing the lines away with the cotton bud/swab.

TIP

If you're nervous, grab a bit of spare fabric and draw some lines, squiggles, even your name onto it, with the water-soluble marker pen. Then, hoop up and sew along the lines for driving practice.

FME STITCHING BASICS

- It is much easier to FME the fabric in one large piece, which is why I recommend cutting the main shapes out after you've done all your stitching. You have more fabric to hold onto, and it fits in the hoop much more easily.
- When you do this sort of technique, don't be too neat with your stitches. Use your drawn outline simply as a guide, as FME is supposed to have a loose, relaxed style.
- On larger items, like this pillow, go over and around stitched lines twice for emphasis (and to cover up any skipped stitches!).
- Sewing machines are a bit funny with the feed dogs down, and will play up a bit if you insist on sewing with only one layer. My advice is to interface what you are embroidering with either a thin fusible wadding/batting (like H630) or a low-loft, sew-in quilting wadding/batting (like #279 80/20 cotton mix). This gives the machine something to bite into, making it run more happily – plus, your design will have a lovely finish. When you hoop up, simply treat the two layers as one.

5 Cut out the front cloud shape (with the smiling face) only. Pin it to the back piece (with the sad face), right sides together, lining up the outlines. Sew the front to the back, leaving a turning gap on the bottom edge. Trim the back piece to match the front.

6 Notch the curves (see page 30) and clip into the contours, being very careful not to cut the stitching.

7 Turn out through the gap. Stuff well with polyester stuffing/fibrefill. Close the gap by hand with ladder stitch (see page 31, Step 6).

EASY FME & INTRODUCTION TO FABRIC TUBES
Sleep Mask

You now have so many skills that, for this make, we'll be looking to fine-tune your new abilities and go into these in a bit more detail.

It is another bagged-out make (see also the technique on page 50), which means that it is largely made inside out; then, at the end, the make is turned out through a gap to hide the raw edges and various joins. I also want to look a bit at which fabrics to choose, how to fit the elastic and, also, why it is often a better idea not to trim the lining immediately.

Let's take those one at a time!

WHAT YOU WILL LEARN:

◎ Working out which fabrics to use

◎ FME: a step up

◎ Incorporating and sewing in elastic

◎ Making a tube

SEWING 101

Working out which fabrics to use

This project is for a sleep mask, so it really matters which fabrics and interfacings we use. Naturally, you'll want to use a pretty fabric for the outer mask part. However, it's important to make the area in front of your eyes as dark as possible, to get that melatonin flowing and help you sleep! A darker fabric will do this. The answer? Simply back your pretty fabric with a darker one. I have used a denim fabric, for interest, but this won't quite cut the mustard. So what's the solution?

You guessed it: interfacing. This will not only introduce structure and cushioning to your eye mask, adding that much-needed comfort around your eyes, but it will also thicken the area in between your main fabrics to make that eye area darker. Saying that, unfortunately, most interfacings come in white or light colours. Even if you can get black or grey, it is not dark enough. To tackle this, I have double interfaced the mask, layering a thinner wadding/batting behind the front fabric where the embroidery is, and then fusing a piece of black felt onto the other side of the denim backing fabric. This felt will act as a faux interfacing, and will cut out any light effectively.

FME: a step up

So why are we discussing FME more if we have already done it? Primarily because this area is worth a deeper delve – there are so many ways you can use FME to decorate your work that it's useful to keep practising it! To recap, you are better off working with your upside down hoop for this because it gives you something with which to steer.

This project is a step up from the last one for a couple of reasons. The stitching for the eyelashes is delicate and – unlike the smile and eyes for the pillow before – you need to make sure the closed eyes and lashes are as symmetrical as possible. My advice on how to tackle both these areas is to check everything before you start stitching, then concentrate and go slowly. This sort of sewing is VERY hard to unpick! My top tip is to photograph your fabric with your phone after you're done. Anomalies show up better in photos.

Incorporating and sewing in elastic

Elastic is the best and most comfortable option for our mask. Don't make it too tight or too loose fitting. If you are making it for yourself, begin by holding the mask onto your face where it would sit and then measure around the back of your head to get an approximate measurement. Then, use this measurement to make your elastic more snug: simply measure in by approximately 2.5cm (1in) on each end and mark the elastic. Effectively, you have now shortened the elastic (without any scary cutting). This gives us some length we can use to feed the elastic through a fabric tube, but it also takes into account its natural recoil: elastic wants to pull out of the stitches, so burying the excess into the layers of fabric that make up the mask ensures it'll be held in place securely.

> ### TIP
>
> In fact, any other item you sew like this with features that will undergo a lot of stress or force – such as the straps of a bag – will need to be similarly 'buried' into the fabric as much as possible. As the edge of the fabric is the weakest point, sewing further in takes the stress away from this weaker area and makes the added feature more secure.

Making a fabric tube

No one wants a sleep mask where you can actually see the elastic on the back! The best way to cover it is with a tube of fabric.

Fabric tubes will come up a lot in your sewing journey, as sewists use these to cover less attractive necessities, like piping cord and elastic, or to use by themselves to create coordinated components for items or garments such as ties, tabs, hanging loops and even delicate bag straps. Making fabric tubes is straightforward, and I'll tackle this in more detail with you in the main pattern instructions.

PATTERN

1 Cut out a 15 x 25cm (6 x 10in) piece from your F8th of contrasting fabric. From your FQ of pretty fabric, cut a 15 x 25cm (6 x 10in) piece and a strip of fabric measuring 6 x 55cm (2½ x 21 ¾in). Set aside the strip of outer fabric for now.

2 Glue the black felt to the wrong side of the contrast fabric piece (at this point, you can insert your dried lavender – tuck a little between the layers before completely fusing the felt to the lining).

3 Fuse the H630 to the wrong side of the 15 x 25cm (6 x 10in) pretty fabric piece. Using the template on Pattern Sheet A, trace and draw the outline of the mask and the closed eyes onto the right side of the pretty fabric (see the technique on page 60 for how to transfer a design). This will be the eye mask front. Don't cut this shape out yet.

4 Set up your machine for free-motion embroidery. Hoop up the eye mask, right side facing, and use the darning foot to embroider the eyes. I have used black thread, but you could play with other colours too! Trim any loose threads from the front and back when finished, and then trim the fabric and interfacing down to the drawn outline. Put this front piece aside.

5 Fold the strip of outer fabric in half lengthways, right sides together [A]. Sew right along the long open side [B], then turn the tube the right way out [C]. A chopstick is your best friend here!

GATHER THESE SUPPLIES:

- Fabric
  - FQ of pretty quilting cotton, for the eye mask front
  - F8th of contrasting quilting cotton, for the eye mask back
- Interfacing
  - 15 x 25cm (6 x 10in) piece of light-weight, non-woven, fusible wadding/batting: I have used H630 by Vlieseline®
  - 15 x 25cm (6 x 10in) piece of black wool felt
- 40cm (16in) length of 2cm (¾in) wide elastic
- Safety pin
- Your essential sewing kit (see page 11), plus darning foot
- Optional: dried lavender (omit if you have allergies)

TEMPLATE ON PATTERN SHEET A

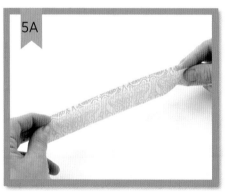

5A

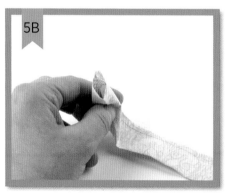

5B

5C

LINE UP, PIN, SEW THEN TRIM

You may have noticed in a few patterns that I have given instructions to leave the lining or backing on things untrimmed until they're sewn in place? Besides the fact that FME is much easier to do on a larger surface, this is also because of friction and fabric creep. Good old physics! Natural friction causes fabric to creep against another piece while you are sewing, so the two will ever so slightly distort (especially on bias edges) or become misaligned. If you are really unlucky, both will happen! The trick is to leave the backing or lining untrimmed until your main shape is sewn and secure. It is not a waste of fabric, because you don't need to leave more than 2cm (¾in) all round. If your top part has crept more than that, it's more likely that you distorted the fabric when pinning. The answer here is to go back a step and be more careful the second time.

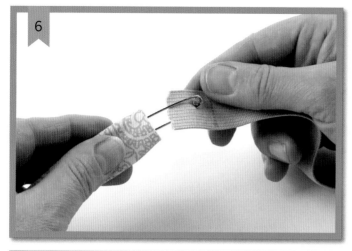

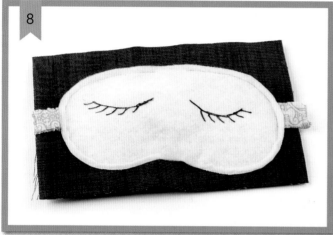

6 Pin one end of elastic to the side of your eye mask front and hold the mask to your face to measure the length of elastic you'll need. Carefully take the mask off then cut the elastic to this back head measurement. With a water-soluble marker pen, mark a 2.5cm (1in) line in from each end of the elastic. Attach a safety pin to one end and thread the elastic through the tube of fabric. Cover the elastic completely with the tube of fabric; the fabric can bunch slightly if necessary, but don't allow it to twist. Secure the fabric and elastic in place with a few stitches. You should be able to see the marked lines on either side of the elastic through the fabric; if not, mark the lines again on both ends onto the fabric. This is your mask strap.

7 There is an indication on the eye mask template where each end of the strap should be sewn. Transfer these marks onto the eye mask front with the water-soluble marker pen, then lay the eye mask strap flat on top of the eye mask front, lining up the marks on the elastic with those on the mask. Pin in place, then sew the band to the mask front at each end, stitching over the marked lines.

8 Pin the mask front to the untrimmed mask back (the contrast fabric piece glued to the black felt), right sides facing. The felt and the interfacing should be on the outside, and the lining and outer fabric touching. When you pin, ensure that the strap is tucked in completely so that it does not get caught in the stitching (except the ends, of course!). The two 2.5cm (1in) bits should be the only parts hanging out. Sew all around the edge of the eyemask, leaving a turning gap in the top.

9 Trim the eye mask back to the size of the eye mask front and notch the curves. Turn out through the gap and gently pull everything into shape. Top-stitch right around the edge, closing the gap as you go. Sleep tight!

Autumn Leaf Garland

Everyone loves a garland or bunting – not only can it cheer up a room, it can tell anyone coming into the room what season it is! Imagine Christmas without some sort of decoration – for me, that would be unthinkable. But I also have garlands for other seasons too, just so that everything is kept relevant.

Well, it seemed a bit clichéd to do a Christmas garland – besides which, there are heaps of those around. I wanted to make an autumn leaf one, one that isn't for Thanksgiving and Halloween (but could certainly be used for both), as a nod to the places in the sewing community where these holidays aren't such a biggie.

SEWING 101

Die-cutting

Now, for this make, you can use the templates provided or you can use a die and die-cutting machine. We have dipped a toe into both, but I would like to spend a few seconds looking at the differences and how you can make the template option better if it is not quite your birthday yet (don't forget to put the die-cutter on the list for that though!).

If you haven't heard of die-cutting before, it is fairly self-explanatory: a die is effectively a mould with a bladed bottom that is in the shape of the design on the mould. You use a die-cutter to press the mould into your chosen material (fabric here, but more commonly paper) and this cuts out the shape of the mould in the fabric. There are so many dies available nowadays it's not even funny – and with it, there are some great bargains to be had too. And did you know that you can almost always swap dies from different manufacturers? Of course you can! Otherwise, magazines would not be able to give away die freebies as they do now and then.

Now, some dies will cut just about everything, and the best of the bunch are the bigger, thicker, steel rule dies like the Bigz range from Sizzix® (shown left). You can cut leather, fabric, felt and almost anything made from paper or card.

The smaller dies you can find are the ones usually given away free with magazines and aimed at paper crafters. Feel free to hijack these! However, be mindful that they are not quite as good at cutting fabric, because they are not so sharp. For this reason, don't choose ones that are too detailed, because the shapes will struggle to come out of the felt or fabric and you will not get a clean cut. A simple shape like a heart or a leaf, and using a thinner felt or fabric, will let these dies work beautifully.

There are so many different die-cutting system machines, so each brand will have a slightly different way of cutting out the fabric to make your appliqué. The brand that I use is Sizzix® and it works by making a 'sandwich' with the two plates (see the glass plates, left) and the die, and laying the fabric in there underneath the die too. Other machines may differ from this, so do make sure you read the instructions on your individual machine first.

Mastering your scissor cutting

So if die-cutting is so great, does that mean that you cannot make this garland or any of the other things demanding a die-cutter in this book? Of course not! People have been doing appliqué for hundreds of years. You just need a good pair of sharp scissors! I have deliberately provided a template for the leaves if you're still doubtful about getting a die-cutter, and you can see this make as an opportunity to sharpen your scissor skills (pun intended).

For this project, and if you haven't done so already, now is the time to invest in a medium-sized pair of scissors: the middle of the blades can conquer the larger areas of cutting, the 'throat' is fabulous for getting around curves with ease, and the tip is perfect for little details. As I mentioned before (see page 11), I love to use Tonic Micro-Serrated scissors for jobs like these.

PATTERN

1 Using either a manual die-cutting machine and leaf die, or medium scissors and the leaf template on Pattern Sheet B, cut out your felt leaves from your different-coloured felt pieces. Follow the instructions on your die-cutting machine; or, if you are cutting with scissors, draw around the leaf template with the water-soluble marker pen and cut.

TIP

Did you know that when you are cutting a curve, it'll cut more smoothly if you hold the scissors still, and move the thing that you are cutting instead? Try it and see. The main thing is never to try to cut a curved bit on a design by making little snips with the scissor tips – the result will be a jagged mess.

2 Lay each coloured leaf onto the grey felt and glue it down. Ensure that you leave at least 2cm (¾in) in between each leaf you stick down, so that you can cut a grey edge around all the leaves later.

GATHER THESE SUPPLIES:

◎ Fabric
- Wool felt, in grey and in different autumnal colours: I am using tan, orange, burgundy and olive green squares, and a metre of grey felt. You need enough for all of the leaves, and if you decide to make this garland longer, you will need more – don't worry, if you buy too much; I guarantee that you will find a use for it!

◎ Black and white baker's twine or cord

◎ Extra strong, all-purpose crafting glue (make sure it is clear drying)

◎ Variegated thread, in an autumn tone: I am using one from Gütermann's multicoloured set

◎ Your essential sewing kit (see page 11), plus darning foot

◎ Optional: manual die-cutting machine plus leaf die

TEMPLATE ON PATTERN SHEET B

WHAT TO DO WHEN THERE ARE NO FABRIC MEASUREMENTS

You may have noticed I have not put in exact amounts for this pattern – this is deliberate. That happens sometimes in a pattern, and it indicates that you can make something shorter or longer, or smaller or larger, as you wish. In this case, it gives you the option of making the banner as long or short as you like. My banner features nine leaves, and is 150cm (59in) long.

3 Set up your sewing machine for free-motion embroidery and insert the variegated thread in the spool holder and bobbin. Sew the veins onto each leaf: begin at the base of each leaf and go almost all the way to the tip before coming back and going over all your stitches again.

TIP

It'll seem odd to sew over your stitches, but this is the charm of FME – it really is like doodling with a pen, and the overlapped stitches give your designs a natural, 'drawn' look.

4 Cut the leaves out, leaving about 5mm (¼in) of grey felt all around as a border.

5 Take your twine or cord and find the centre. Attach one of the leaves here with all-purpose glue, running a line at the back of the leaf stem and looping it around the twine to stick and secure. Clipping foldback/bulldog clips over the folded stems will help keep them in place while the glue is drying.

6 Repeat this process all the way along the twine. Whatever length you choose, allow 30cm (12in) at each end for making your loop and hanging – if necessary, lay the leaves out beforehand and mark the placement of each one prior to sticking them on – I placed the leaves approximately 20cm (8in) apart. Once all the leaves are attached, knot the ends of the cord to form hanging loops.

TIP

You can use many types of twine, rope or cord for this project – macramé cord, for example, is great for garlands. If you cannot find a cord with the right thickness, consider plaiting some garden jute string – this looks wonderfully rustic.

CHAPTER 3: APPLIQUÉ & SURFACE STITCHING

69

la vie
est belle

Well, by now you are no stranger to appliqué or FME. One of my favourite things to do with it is to write with thread: it is a great way to add interest to a project, and you can write phrases (as we are here) or people's names to personalize a gift.

As writing is cursive and the flowers are all circles or long ovals, this make is all about curves. It is a good practice piece as, once you have this technique down, your thread writing skills – and pretty much any FME you encounter after this – will be a breeze.

WHAT YOU WILL LEARN:

◎ Writing with thread
◎ Raggy appliqué
◎ Transferring a pattern

SEWING 101

Writing with thread

We'll be stitching *La vie est belle* ('Life is beautiful') into our fabric for a simple, beautiful hoop to display in your home. Again, you'll be working with your upside-down hoop to give you something with which to steer. Always allow plenty of fabric for you to stitch on, especially if you're still getting to grips with the technique, so don't be too stingy when cutting it out before embroidering (unless you are using the very last piece of a favourite fabric which cannot be bought any more; in these situations, wait until you have had a bit more practice, and use a smaller hoop, too).

Even though we won't see the back of our embroidery, I advise interfacing your fabric – especially as we'll be using quilting cotton to stitch into. Quilting cotton is a relatively thin fabric, and the problem here is that a sewing machine set up for FME does not sew happily into a single layer of fabric and can sometimes play up a bit. The interfacing will help it to mind its manners as you write with your thread.

Posture plays its part, too, when tackling more complex shapes in FME. Don't sit back in your chair, slumped like a sack of potatoes. Sit up and sit forward, and allow the hoop to become an extension of your body. Instead of moving just your wrists, or from the elbows, move from the shoulders; this will help you achieve graceful curves.

Think this advice is a bit overkill? Try it and see the difference! The shoulders employ more muscles (meaning that you are not just targeting one or two and allowing them to become fatigued or injured) and you are using larger ones too, giving you greater control over your work.

Raggy appliqué

In most of the projects so far, we have taken great care to cut out and FME our shapes for appliqué. This isn't the case with **raggy appliqué**! Known also as 'raggy-edge appliqué', this is one of the easiest appliqué methods to use as there is no fiddly sewing or cutting and no fear of fraying the edges – instead, you want them to fray! However, to ensure the frayed edges of your cut fabric do not travel too far, which could spoil your work, you will need to FME close to the edge of the shape – hence why your FME flowers petals will stay mostly within the fabric circles and the stitching is nice and wide.

Naturally, to make our flowers look like flowers, the curves in this piece will require a bit of scrap practice. The technique is exactly the same as for the cloud and the eye mask but this time, whole curves are needed, which can be a bit trickier.

Of course, this project is an opportunity to return to our button stash and select some cute ones for our flower centres! For a beginner, these are particularly useful to add as buttons also can help to hide any messy stitching in the centre, which is the place where your embroidering will start and stop.

PATTERN

1 Fuse the H630 onto the wrong side of your F8th of fabric.

2 Using the water-soluble marker pen, draw around the outside of the embroidery hoop onto the interfaced fabric (alternatively, use the circle size suggested on the pattern, found on Pattern Sheet B). This is your working area, and it'll help you work out how much room you have to place the rest of the features on the design.

3 Using the pattern template (or your creativity), cut out small circles from your floral and patterned fabric scraps to make the flower heads. These do not have to be perfect and exactly round! A wobbly edge around your flower heads looks quite natural.

4 Adhere the flower heads to the centre of your circle of fabric with a fabric glue stick, using the pattern template as a guide. Draw the words and petal details onto the fabric with your water-soluble marker pen, to follow as you sew later (see the technique box on page 60 for advice on transferring the design).

5 Set up your machine for free-motion embroidery. Hoop up your fabric with the design in the centre. Embroider the words and flowers. When complete, snip the threads at the front and back of the fabric.

TIP

Of course, don't discount the idea of drawing your own words and flower designs. This will leave you with a unique make as it'll be your handwriting on it rather than mine. If you wish, practise drawing on a scrap of paper and see how you go, then trace your words onto the fabric with a water-soluble marker pen and get stitching!

GATHER THESE SUPPLIES:

- ◉ Fabric
  - F8th of textured quilting cotton: ideally, it should not have too much patterning to allow the embroidery to stand out
  - 30cm (12in) square of felt, for the back: I tend to keep the colours that I am not so fond of from a variety pack for this job
  - Scraps of floral and patterned quilting cotton, for the flower heads
- ◉ Interfacing
  - 25cm (10in) square of light-weight, non-woven, fusible wadding/batting: I have used H630 by Vlieseline®
- ◉ Three little buttons
- ◉ Spray bottle filled with water and a cotton bud/swab
- ◉ 24cm (9½in) embroidery hoop – you use this one for the working and mounting afterwards
- ◉ Hot-glue gun and glue or extra strong, all-purpose crafting glue
- ◉ Your essential sewing kit (see page 11), plus darning foot
- ◉ Optional: craft knife

TEMPLATE ON PATTERN SHEET B

6 Remove the removable marker lines and mount the picture in the large hoop. Hand-sew the buttons to the flower centres with a needle and thread. Next, trim the excess fabric around the hoop until you have a 2.5cm (1in) rounded edge all the way around.

> **TIP**
>
> Remove the marker lines by spraying the fabric with cold water and rubbing the lines away with the cotton bud/swab.

7 Take your needle and thread again. Using a rather long running stitch, sew all around the edge of the excess fabric using a generous seam allowance. What you are making is a 'gathering' stitch. When you get back to the start, pull the thread until you gather the fabric behind the hoop. Tie the thread off to secure the gathers.

8 Get the hot-glue gun out and your square piece of felt. Carefully run a line of glue along the frame of the hoop, pressing your square of felt on top as you go. Make sure you stretch the felt, too, as you work around the hoop, to keep it nice and taut.

> **TIP**
>
> If you find that hot glue is too quick to set, opt for that strong, all-purpose craft glue instead (see page 13), which will give you a longer working time. For this option, simply run a line of glue around the back of the frame, lay the felt on the back and then sit a couple of books on top of the hoop until it is dry.

9 Once the glue has dried, trim the excess felt away as neatly as you can with scissors. Alternatively, lay the frame onto a self-healing cutting mat and glide a craft knife around the edge to trim. You've done it!

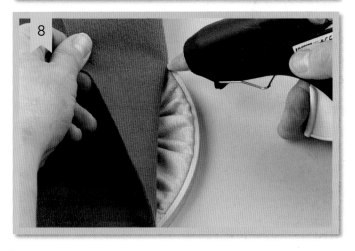

There's so much satisfaction in a job well done: not only have you drawn flowing words in needle and thread, you've made a lovely decorative hoop with a neat and professional finish.

Koala Toy

Making toys is great fun, and you can take it to any level of complexity, but because this is a beginner's book I have a really simple pattern for a teddy with a difference – this little guy is a koala! A stuffed animal toy of some sort is welcomed by just about anyone, and this eucalyptus-loving dude is a nod to my Australian roots.

I love the fact that, with a simple change or two to a basic pattern, you can change the whole look of your happy, traditional bear. So use this design as a way of seeing how to create your own favourite bears – for example, if you tweak the pattern template by shrinking the ears and moving them further up the head, adjusting the size of the nose and then changing the colours to different shades of brown, you can create a fuzzy grizzly bear!

This make is also a good opportunity to explore the possibilities of upcycled fabrics: this bear would work well made in 'rougher' fabrics like denim and tweed, which you can snap up from charity/thrift/op-shops.

SEWING 101

Making toys

A lot of soft toys you see out and about tend to include things called **gussets** – these are extra shapes of fabric (usually oval, triangular or diamond shaped) that are added to the seam of a toy (or in dressmaking, a garment) to expand a seam to add contouring and three-dimensionality. A nice way of understanding this is to think of a simple drawing of a diamond: by adding little 'facets' inside, you can suggest a more three-dimensional shape.

However, you can still achieve a lovely design with your toy without the necessity of a gusset and, if anything, there's something wonderfully simple about making a 2D-style character – making this a project for which you are more than ready.

The things to remember as you stitch your little guy are the appropriate clipping and notching of the curves so that they do not pucker, and to fill the parts of the koala really well with stuffing: quite often, the undoing of these projects is to under fill them, which makes them floppy and sad. The arms especially need to be quite firm.

WARNING: MAKING TOYS FOR KIDS

Because this make is primarily intended for little ones, I have not used buttons, beads or safety eyes. You could replace the FME eyes with these but remember, such additions (even the safety eyes) can be chewed or pulled until they come off, and then they present a real choking hazard. You will know the recipient best, but as a general rule I would advise against using anything other than appliqué and FME.

Layering appliqué: building a picture in fabric... in the right order!

Before we get to the actual pattern, let's consider appliqué patterns that have more than one layer. As you can see from the pattern, this toy has a small mouth which is tucked under the bottom of the nose. So how do you know which bits of a complicated design go on top of another, and which go underneath? With the pillow (see page 58), the garland (see page 66) and the hoop (see page 70), we only had one layer of appliqué to think about; with this pattern, there are two. For other similar patterns with lots of features, there can be several layers! Therefore, it is quite important that you lay them out in the correct order.

The answer to tackling these multiple layers is to look carefully at the pattern template provided. The 'picture' is usually built from the bottom up, and quite often the layered appliqué is represented by solid and dotted lines: the dotted line is the part of the appliqué piece that will sit under another piece; the solid line on the same piece is the part that will stay visible, or on top of all the layers. Overlapping appliqué like this is a nice addition to a make; besides adding more complexity to a simple design, it suggests more dimension without the faff of a gusset.

With all layered appliqué, fabric glue will be your BFF! However, make sure you lay out the appliqué pieces first before gluing anything down, to ensure you've got the order correct.

FME to secure shapes

The details on this make – the paws, nose, chin and eyes – are secured or made entirely with FME. For the appliqué features, you simply follow the contours of the pieces and sew close to the edge, as you're really only using FME as a way to secure them. For the eyes, sew in the same area a few times so that you get cute, small, French knot-like dots. Don't worry if this all sounds confusing – details like these will always be on the pattern.

PATTERN

1 Fuse the H630 to the wrong side of the FQ. Then, using the templates on Pattern Sheet A, draw the koala outlines onto the right side of the main fabric: draw two koala bodies – one for the front and one for the back – and four arm pieces, remembering to mirror image two of them to ensure there is a left and right arm. Cut out the koala back only – you need to leave the koala front and arms uncut to make FME easier later.

2 Use the template to transfer the feature shapes (nose, chin and paw pads) onto your scraps of grey felt, then cut your felt features. Lay out your felt features onto the koala outline, using the template as a guide. Once you are happy with how they sit, start gluing them down: glue the bottom layer first, followed by the top layer. When this is done, draw in the eyes.

3 Set up your machine for free-motion embroidery. Hoop up your fabric, then embroider over the felt features: for the nose, chin and paw pads, simply embroider around the edge a couple of times. For the eyes, FME in the same spot over and over again to create a solid circle of stitching.

GATHER THESE SUPPLIES:

- Fabric
  - FQ of textured quilting cotton, for the koala body: I have used denim
  - Scraps of grey felt, for the nose, chin and paws: I used about 20cm (8in) square each of the light and dark grey
  - Long scrap of patterned fabric, for the scarf: I have used jersey knit as it has a nice stretch to it
- Interfacing
  - 46 x 56cm (18¼ x 22in) piece of light-weight, non-woven, fusible wadding/batting: I have used H630 by Vlieseline®
- Polyester stuffing/fibrefill
- Your essential sewing kit (see page 11), plus darning foot

TEMPLATES ON PATTERN SHEET A

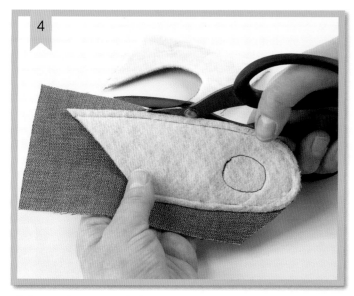

4 Cut out the arms with the paw pads attached, then sew them right sides together to their corresponding pieces, leaving the ends furthest from the paw open. Cut out your arm pieces, keeping the angled top edge.

5 Notch the seam allowance around the curve of the paw then turn the arm the right way out. Fill well with polyester stuffing/fibrefill. Repeat for the other arm.

TIP

Notice that the sides of each arm are not equal in length, and drawn so that the bit near the body is cut on an angle? This angle allows the arm to follow the contours of the body when you attach it later.

TIP

Pack the arms tightly with stuffing, but do not fill them all the way to the end – leave approx. 2cm (¾in) space near the 'socket' end. Otherwise, this would make the arms too stiff, and they would stick out and look odd.

6 On the template there are marks indicating where the arms are to be attached to the body. If these have not been transferred already onto your main fabric, do this now. Pin an arm onto its respective side on the koala body front, between the marks: to do this, fold over the 'baggy' end of the arm first by approx. 5mm (¼in) and pin along this folded edge, right along the drawn outline. Make sure the arm is pinned towards the body and the paw pad is facing down. Sew along the pinned fold line. Repeat with the other arm.

7 Tuck the arms well in towards the body and pin. Place the cut-out koala back piece onto the koala front, right sides together. Sew right around the outer edge, leaving a small turning gap along one side of the neck. Trim the koala front to the same size as the koala back then clip and notch the seam allowance where necessary. Turn out through the gap. Stuff the koala well and close the gap by hand using ladder stitch (see page 31, Step 6).

8 Take your scarf fabric and tie it around your koala's neck. This covers any visible hand-stitching around the neck and adds a little character to your toy! For my scarf, I cut strip of fabric approximately 8 x 40cm (3⅛ x 15¾in).

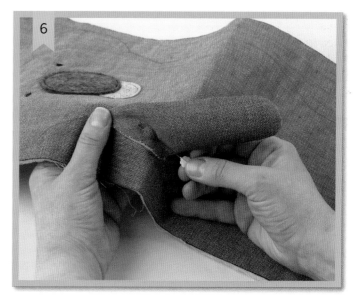

It might feel as though we are leaving the world of regular sewing for a bit in this section, but bear with me: quilting and patching is simply sewing's sister. The concepts for both techniques are actually quite simple, and by the end of this chapter you will have all the skills that you need to make a quilt of any size. There will be one or two specialized things to learn, but these really are small variations on what you've already tackled!

Saying that, there is a world of difference between making a super-king quilt and a mug rug, so if it is all the same to you I think that we will start our journey with a mug rug!

SEWING 101

Quilting and patching 101

So what is quilting and patching? You might be surprised to learn that they are two very different things. A lot of people slam the two together and refer to them generally as 'quilting', and certainly it's OK to refer to both as 'quilting' if you use the two techniques together. However, let's clear up the difference between the two first, as my OCD won't let us continue otherwise.

Patching or **patchwork** is the art of making patterns with fabric. My father once asked why we buy perfectly good fabric and cut it all up, only to sew it back together again. Bless his cotton socks, he missed the point entirely. However, he did give us a pretty good definition of patchwork! We DO cut perfectly good fabric up and we DO sew it back together again – but we piece and sew it back together again differently. There are libraries full of books written on the variations of patchwork, way beyond the scope of this book, but patching is effectively all about making patterns with fabric shapes. Quilting is the part where you take your patched panel, layer it onto other materials and then sew the whole lot together. In the sewing world, this is called a **quilt sandwich**. Ahem. I had better explain.

A quilt sandwich has three layers: backing fabric (the back or underneath bit of the quilt), interfacing (usually wadding/ batting, to give depth, squishiness and warmth to your quilt) and the patchwork top (the decorative bit of your quilt). Sewing these three layers together is what makes a quilt different from a blanket! The sewing of the three layers – known as **quilting** – can be done in lots of ways to make your top panel of fabric more decorative: you can sew simple lines, Chanel-style diamonds (see page 88–91 if this takes your fancy), squares or such a work of art in stitching that you forget to look at the patchwork.

What is a block?

Patchwork is almost always organized into things called **blocks**. Imagine sewing lots of patches together to form a square design – this is a 'block'. If little patches are cut and sewn in a specific way to form a mini design within your block – such as two triangular patches of different fabrics sewn together to form a small square – these mini designs are known as **units**. The top layer of a quilt is often made with lots of blocks to make an overall design. Often your pattern will give instructions on how

to make just one block, and then will tell you how many more of these to make. This means that the rest of the blocks will be the same as this one, and to make the whole patchwork quilt top you simply repeat the process and sew them all together.

How to measure for patching

You've conquered 'FQ and 'F8th', so let's look at some new terminology that you'll find in the realms of patching. Often your pattern will tell you to cut your fabric (often a fat quarter) into strips –

by —cm (—in) x WOFQ **or** LOFQ

This means that you will need to measure and cut out strips from your fat quarter at a specific width, then the length is either the width of the fat quarter (WOFQ) – the shortest side of an FQ, or the length of fat quarter (LOFQ) – the longest side of an FQ. You will see this a lot, and not only does it avoid lots of measuring but it's a way of getting the most from your fabric. Occasionally, Log Cabin block patterns will tell you how long to make each strip, but this is boring and unnecessary: after marking the first two pieces, both of which have to be square, you only need to work out the width.

Which wadding?

Speaking of wadding (or batting, depending on where you live), you have a few choices. We have briefly talked about high- and low-loft interfacings, and when it comes to quilting and patching this is another time when the type of wadding/batting is relevant. For quilting, a high-loft (thicker) wadding/batting tends to be used, as it gives the quilt more volume. However, you can do without this in a mug rug! As you'll see later, my favourite go-to wadding/batting for most of my quilted items is a low-loft, sew-in interfacing (such as #279 80/20 cotton mix by Vlieseline®), as it is strong, beautifully even and very versatile. However, in this case, we'll be sticking with our light-weight, fusible friend here – the H630. As we'll be bagging out (see page 50) our make, we need to use a fusible wadding/batting, as a sew-in can shift and make ugly bunches when the make is turned the right way out. Once you have turned through the mug rug, we'll use top-stitching (i.e. quilting) to make sure that interfacing stays put.

How to walk-the-walk with a walking foot

I want to introduce you to a piece of sewing-machine kit which, if you haven't got already (and do check the depths of the I-won't-ever-use-whatever-this-is box) is worth tootling out to buy. Also known as a dual-feed foot, a walking foot is a wonderful piece of equipment that allows you to feed through and sew lots of layers together without them bunching up and distorting – perfect for quilting! So how does it differ from a regular presser foot? A universal foot helps to take fabric through the machine but only very lightly – most of the pulling action is only going on underneath the fabric, through the feed dogs. (Remember these from all that FME? See page 59 for a reminder.) A walking foot, however, creates a feed dog-like effect on the top fabric too, and this allows all the layers in the quilt sandwich to be taken evenly through the machine, stopping fabric shift and reducing puckering. Here's a rule: whenever you have more than two layers to sew, use a walking foot.

Typical walking foot; used mostly for quilting.

The good news is that, if your machine doesn't come with one, a walking foot doesn't usually cost a huge amount. I will keep adding to your knowledge about these feet as we go along too, so don't think for one moment that this a foot you'll use only once or twice. For now, get one (or find it in the box) and have a play with it.

Sneaky hardware no. 2

Now finally (and I really mean it this time), I want to show you something (else) to which I have become a bit addicted: Chicago screws. Sounds a bit like a 1920s gangster torture device, right? Actually, they are a remnant of the publishing industry, once used to hold large amounts of paper together. They consist of two parts: a shank part and a screw part.

All nice, I know, but why am I telling you about this? Well, like many other things, this is something that we can hijack and use for sewing. These screws are easy to assemble, strong and – thanks to the various different shank lengths you can buy – can slot through lots of fabric layers. Simply punch a hole in the place where you want the screw to go, pop the flat-ended section through and then use a screwdriver to attach the other section to the back. The screws are supposed to have the screw mark facing inwards, but occasionally I like to have it facing outwards and use it as a feature.

The joy of these guys is that you can create the look of a rivet without using one: you don't have to hammer Chicago screws as you have to with rivets, and so avoid the struggle of removing a bent rivet – a real boon for beginners. In addition, Chicago screws are cheap and sold in decent-sized packets online.

PATTERN

The project this time is made with one of the most classic and timeless blocks – the **Log Cabin**. There are many different variations of this one and they are all beautiful. Log Cabin patching is well worth learning to do if you're a beginner because you do not have to match your seams. (Heads up – seam matching, plus quilt binding, awaits you in the next chapter...) In addition, the small size of this mug rug means you can practise your quilting lines on a small scale.

1 From two of the pretty fabric F8ths/FQs, cut a 5cm (2in) square. With the remaining fabric and from the other pretty fabric F8ths/FQs, cut one strip measuring 5cm (2in) wide x LOF8th.

> **TIP**
>
> To avoid too much waste, only cut one strip at a time from each F8th/FQ. This will work brilliantly if you're cutting from scraps of fabric.

GATHER THESE SUPPLIES:

- Fabric
  - Five F8ths or FQs of pretty quilting cotton, for the top – your scraps are your best friends here too!
  - F8th of contrasting quilting cotton, for the backing
  - Scrap of leather
- Interfacing
  - 56cm (22in) square of light-weight, non-woven, fusible wadding/batting: I have used H630 by Vlieseline®
- 5mm (¼in) brass Chicago screw, plus flat head screwdriver
- Awl (or see 'Optional')
- Your essential sewing kit (see page 11), plus walking foot
- Optional: revolving leather-punch pliers

2 Sew the two squares right sides together. Press the seam allowance flat. Next, take one strip (ideally one in a different fabric from the squares) and sew it to the left of the first two squares in the same way. As you can see, it hangs over quite a way. Trim it off so it is level with the square and put the offcut aside.

PRESSING YOUR PATCHES

The smaller you cut the patch pieces (and some patterns can be really intricate), the less strength the fabric has and the more likelihood of it becoming misshapen and unusable. Pressing will sort this out!

A Log Cabin can be finger pressed because the strips are cut on the straight of grain. So, after each strip addition, finger press for speed and ease; you'll then iron the whole block at the end. (For more information on finger pressing, see 'Finger pressing' lingo box on page 31 or 'Seam pressing for quilting' techniques box on page 56.)

TIP

When it comes to cutting and trimming your patch strips, I recommend using a rotary cutter, quilting ruler and self-healing cutting mat. Drawing out the dimensions of your strips on the fabric with a water-soluble marker pen and then cutting with scissors is OK, but is less precise and will take longer.

3 Take another strip, place it along the top of one of the squares and above one short end of the sewn strip. This placement matters because the Log Cabin block must be joined in a particular way, like spiralling strips applied clockwise around the centre squares that increase the size of the block. Repeat the process in Step 2, of sewing the strip to the other pieces right sides together and then trimming off the excess. Continue to sew the strips in the same way, working round the central strips, until you have made a block that measures 20cm (8in) square – or, as I did, stop a little earlier to make a rectangular mug rug.

TIP

You'll notice you'll have some offcuts by piecing your Log Cabin together in this way. You can keep these offcuts for future quilting projects (so don't throw them away!) but, normally, you would plan your colours and their lengths a little more beforehand: quite often an offcut from an outer strip is perfect for using as the squares in the centre of the block (as you can see in the photo on page 78), which means less cutting and much more economical fabric usage. The only time this won't work is when you are working to a strict colour pattern.

4 Press the finished top. Fuse a piece of H630 to the wrong side.

5 Cut a slightly larger piece of backing fabric from your remaining F8th. Centre and pin the fused top panel to the untrimmed backing fabric, right sides together.

6 Sew around the perimeter of the mug rug, leaving a turning gap. Trim the backing fabric and interfacing down to the size of the patchwork top. Clip across the corners and turn out through the gap. Close the gap and press lightly so that the edges are perfect.

7 Set up your machine with the walking foot. Quilt the mat in concentric squares or rectangles, working from the outer edge – about 1cm ($^3/_8$in) in – and continuing until you almost reach the centre.

TIP

As you quilt (which is actually just glorified top-stitching), keep an eye on the backing fabric to ensure that it is nice and taut. Even with the walking foot in place, the fabric can become a turncoat and bunch up now and then as you sew.

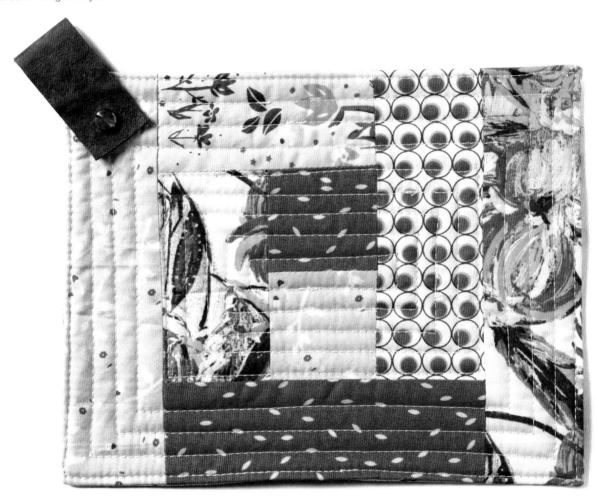

TIP

If the thought of trying to sew evenly spaced lines is nerve-wracking, you can buy a quilting guide for your walking foot. This is inserted into the back of the foot, and can be shifted to the left or right to accommodate your particular seam allowance and quilt pattern. By adjusting and following this guide, you can maintain an even distance between quilt lines. Alternatively, you could take the time to draw out your lines with a water-soluble marker pen. Either way, remember practice makes perfect!

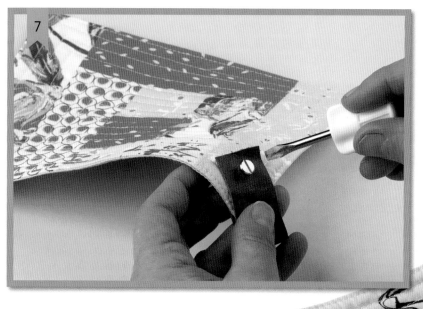

7

8 Now to finish off! Trim the leather tab to 2.5cm x 10cm (1 x 4in) in size. Using an awl or revolving leather-punch pliers, punch a hole on each short side of the leather, large enough to admit the shank of your Chicago screw. Punch a hole in the top left-hand corner of the mug rug. Line up the fabric and one of the leather holes, and insert one part of your Chicago screw. Fold over the other end of your leather tab to the other side of the mug rug so the hole lines up, then push the other part of the Chicago screw through the hole. Using the screw driver, tighten the screw to secure.

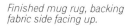

Finished mug rug, backing fabric side facing up.

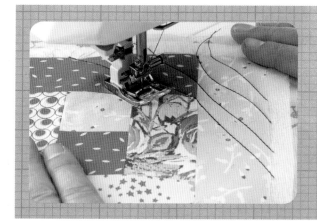

QUILTING VARIATION: WAVE

The Log Cabin suits square-like quilting patterns, owing to its shape, but there's no reason why you couldn't mix this up! One of my favourite quilting patterns to use is my signature free-wave stitching. Increase the length of stitch, then simply work waving lines diagonally across your patchwork top, gently twisting the fabric as you sew to create the 'wavy' effect. This is a perfect if you're new to quilting, and nervous about the prospect of sewing evenly spaced, symmetrical lines.

Mod Place Mat

I do hope, with the last project, that you can see the attraction of patchwork and quilting. Let's just go with the herd from here on in and call it quilting – now that you know the difference, of course. There are so many possibilities by combining these two together, and hopefully this has inspired you to keep on looking for new ideas!

In this project, I want to demonstrate some new technical patchworking know-how, this time with another method of joining your patchwork pieces together. There are debates raging over how this should be done, so I'm going to make it my mission to show you the one that I find the easiest.

WHAT YOU WILL LEARN:

◉ Matching and joining patchwork points
◉ The seam pressing debate
◉ Binding a quilt
◉ Homemade bias binding

SEWING 101

Matching and joining patchwork points

So far in your sewing journey, you've simply joined your fabrics together and haven't needed to give too much consideration to their placement apart from making sure they create the final intended shape of the item. However, now we're delving into a slightly tricker patching technique of **matching and joining points**. Joining points refers to the part of a block where several patch pieces meet at a central intersection. This meeting point must be as perfect as you can get it, and it's a technique like this where quilters can really exhibit their skills.

Have a look at the middle of the place mat shown opposite, and you will see what I mean. There are four squares to begin with and we sew them together to make what is called a **four-patch block** – one of the most basic patchwork blocks and well worth learning. The pro with this block design is that it is super simple; the con is that because it's super simple, you have nowhere to hide from technical errors. The intersection in the middle must be spot on or it will draw your eye. I will show you how to do this later.

✗ *See how the four points don't meet together in the middle? This doesn't look neat, and is something to avoid.*

✓ *This is what you want to aim for – corners that meet perfectly in the middle.*

The seam pressing debate

Once you've matched up your points and sewn your patches together, you press the seams to keep them flat for quilting. I like to press my seams flat or 'open' (which you've seen before, in Step 4b on page 47) but there is another method called **nesting the seams**. This is when seams for one unit are pressed to the left, and the other is pressed to the right. This means when the two are joined there is a nice, neat, flat intersection.

Now we have a hotly debated topic on our hands. Which way is the right way? Well, in my opinion (and only my opinion) **pressing the seams flat** is the best because it reduces bulk. Especially once your get into intensive quilting, where you may find some blocks with as many as eight layers of fabric at an intersection, pressing the seams to alternate sides (i.e. nesting the seams) would be far too bulky, and could create a point of friction that, over time, will wear a hole in the fabric. Pressing the seams flat makes the fabric less visible on the right side and wears better too. Saying that, it is still worth learning both methods, because some quilts may suit one method better than the other.

Binding a quilt

There's a crucial difference between this make and the mug rug from the last chapter. The mug rug was 'bagged out' – sewn together with the right sides facing, so that all you needed to do was turn it through a gap the right way out to hide the (ugly) raw edges. The difference this time is that the quilt sandwich will be built with the wrong sides facing, so you see the 'nice sides' throughout the sewing process. This is actually the usual way to quilt – you could not possibly bag out a super-king quilt! Plus, interfacing for quilts tends to be thicker, making it harder to bag out. No, we have to layer the sandwich as follows – backing fabric face down, then the wadding/batting on top, then the patched top sitting on both these layers, facing up. No turning is needed.

So here's what you'll need to do. To cover the raw edges of your top panel, wadding/batting and backing fabric, you will need to use bias binding. You can buy this, as you know by now, but let's mix things up here and make our own! This is perfect if you want a specific colour or fabric. And did you know that you can get a little over 7m (approximately 7½ yards) of bias binding from one FQ!?

PATTERN

1 From each F8th cut two 15.5cm (6in) squares. You will have four squares in total.

2 Take two contrasting squares and sew them together. Then, take the other two and sew these together too. There are now two double square units. Press flat or nest the seams (see also page 85).

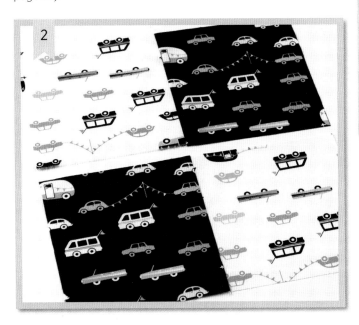

(see also page 85)

GATHER THESE SUPPLIES:

◉ Fabric
  - Two F8ths of contrasting quilting cotton, for the patched top panel
  - FQ of coordinating quilting cotton, for backing the place mat
  - FQ of corresponding solid, for making the bias binding
◉ Interfacing
  - 33cm (13in) square of soft, light-weight, cotton/polyester mix, sew-in wadding/batting: I have used #279 80/20 cotton mix by Vlieseline®
◉ Dinner plate (or see 'Optional')
◉ Your essential sewing kit (see page 11), plus walking foot
◉ Optional: sewing gauge, bias tape maker

WHICH SIDE TO NEST THE SEAMS?

If you choose to press the seams to one side, always press them towards the dark side! This is so you don't see a shadow through the fabric. If both fabrics are light, this is another argument in favour of pressing them open – it makes the shadow even on both sides.

3 Now to match the seams! There are two options, depending on whether you've pressed the seams flat [A] or nested them [B]: lay the two units on top of each other, right sides facing, so contrasting fabrics are touching one another. Match up the seams as accurately as you can, then pin the two units together to secure. Sew the two units together, across the seams.

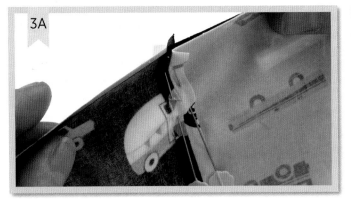

Matching the seams for units with pressed-open seams.

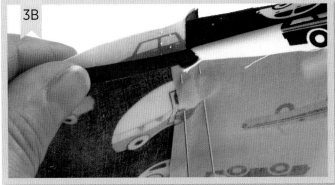

Matching the seams for units with nested seams. See how they have been pressed to the darker side?

4 Lay the pressed backing fabric onto a flat surface, pattern side facing down, followed by the wadding/batting and then the pressed four-patch block on top, pattern side facing up. Pin so that movement is restricted. This is your quilt sandwich.

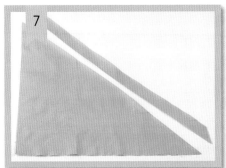

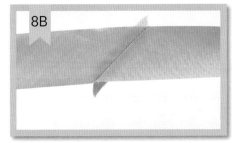

5 Set up your machine with the walking foot. Using my signature wave pattern (see page 83), quilt random waves across the whole of your pinned sandwich, working diagonally from one corner to another.

6 Using a dinner plate or sewing gauge and a water-soluble marker pen, draw a circle onto your four-patch top, approx. 28cm (11in) in diameter. Cut out the circle and set aside.

7 Now for your handmade bias binding! With your remaining FQ, cut strips on the diagonal measuring 3.5cm (1½in) wide. Repeat from one corner to the other. Don't trim the triangular ends straight – you'll need these!

8 Take two strips and lay them on top of each other, right sides together and overlapping the ends at right angles. Now sew a regular seam from one corner to the other [**A**]. When you open out, you will have a straight strip that is joined on the bias [**B**]. Trim the triangle ends so they sit flush. Repeat this process with the remaining strips, joining them all together to create one long length of bias tape.

9 To finish your binding, fold it in half lengthways and iron a crease [**A**]. Then, either manually press the edges of the tape in towards the crease, or run your tape through a bias tape maker [**B**], pressing with the iron as you go to secure.

10 Apply your bias binding in the same way as you did for the slippers (see Steps 10 and 11 on page 57): lay one long edge of the binding, folded edges facing up, along the raw edge of your place mat on the four-patch top. Using a normal seam allowance, sew all the way around. Flip the mat over and fold the bias binding over to the other side. Hand-sew the other edge of the binding in place with ladder stitch to create a neat, finished edge.

TIP

If you need to add another length of bias tape, treat the end to be joined and the end of the new length as you would treat the beginning and ends of bias tape – see the technique box on page 57 for more details.

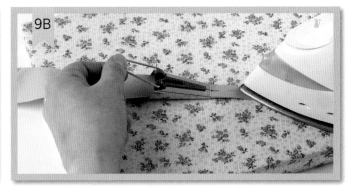

Pot Holder

Can I let you in on a little secret? You don't have to have made a patchwork top to be able to quilt. Seriously.

Say you have a wonderful fabric that you have printed yourself, or a fabric with a beautiful but larger-scale pattern; you don't want to cut it up because cutting it up and sewing it back together again will spoil the pattern, or make it harder to see. In this situation, you need something that we call **wholecloth quilting**. That is actually just a fancy-schmancy way of saying you've quilted the whole of one type of fabric, and not made a patchwork pattern to begin with.

This is a perfect quilting technique for beginner machine quilters, as it's not only a great way of practising your quilting stitches but you have the pleasure of making a quilt without cutting up or reshaping lots of little strips and scraps of fabric. It's a very versatile technique that can be used on a wide variety of items; we're going to put it to good use with a pot holder.

SEWING 101

Chanel/diamond quilting pattern

For our pot holder, we're going to use another classic quilting pattern. Known as the **Chanel** or **diamond quilting pattern**, you simply sew straight lines at a 45-degree angle all across your fabric one way, then sew them again at a 45-degree angle the other, allowing the second series of lines to intersect with the first. The angle means that you will have your squares *en pointe* like a diamond. *Et voila! C'est Chanel!* Sometimes the simplest quilting pattern is best – Coco Chanel knew this when she decided to use this classic diamond pattern on everything.

How to print your own fabric

Since I mentioned to you earlier about printing your own fabric, would you like to have a go? I have a method that is really easy. It's actually a cheat's method but it works well and is washable, so gives you everything that you need in a fabric destined to be used for sewing!

You'll need a nice piece of interesting textured but plain fabric, 'normal' paper craft stamps (yep, you heard me) and stamping ink. I am using a linen and cotton blend fabric, as this will give me a nice textured background (but slow up the creasing and fraying) and both are natural fibres – synthetic fabrics can affect the inks. For the stamps, you can (finally) use those ones that come with your craft magazine! In fact, some of the cheaper stamps are better than the highly detailed rubber stamps, but do try to choose a stamp that doesn't have too many fussy details or shallow areas. With the stamping ink you'll need to make sure it won't wash out – my favourite brand is Ranger Archival™ as it is permanent.

Of course, you can use 'proper' inks and hand carve your own stamps if that floats your boat, but to begin with, using a great quality permanent ink and any old stamp which tests well on a scrap of your intended fabric will get the job done.

Joining interfacing

Interfacing, like regular fabric, produces scraps (as I'm sure you've discovered...). I wanted to reassure you that they can also (in most cases) be reused. As luck would have it, the quilting wadding/batting we'll use for this pot holder is one of the easiest to reuse as it's nice and thick.

To join your interfacing, start by trimming the edges you intend to stitch together, so that they're as straight as possible. Then, butt them up together before using a zigzag stitch to join the two pieces – simple.

One thing to remember is never to overlap your interfacing to join pieces – butt them as close as you can only. Overlapping will cause a ridge on the quilt front, which is not only visible but also forms a high point which may wear down the top fabric and cause a hole over time.

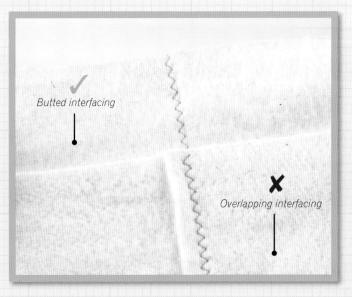

Butted interfacing

Overlapping interfacing

PATTERN

1 Begin by making 90cm (35½in) of bias binding, using your FQ of solid fabric. (If you need a reminder of how to make your own bias binding, see Steps 7–9 on page 87.) Set this aside.

2 From your textured fabric, cut a piece approx. 17cm (6¾in) square – this will be the hand pocket of the pot holder. Use this to help you cut out another square, slightly larger in size. This will be the backing fabric for your hand pocket. Print your focal stamp design (here, the large cactus) onto the centre of your hand pocket fabric. Depending on your stamp, you may need multiple colours and have to work in a particular order. For my large cactus, I stamped the main plant first [A], followed by the foliage around it [B], and finished with the pot [C].

TIP

Play around with a scrap of the same fabric to see how much ink and pressure to use. Fabric sucks the ink up in a way that paper does not, so it is good to get a feel for what you need – it is very difficult to get a good second print if the first one goes wrong.

GATHER THESE SUPPLIES:

- Fabric
  - FQ of textured fabric, for the outer: I have used a linen/cotton blend
  - FQ of solid for bias binding: I opted for a green solid to harmonize with my cacti
  - Scrap of tan leather
- Interfacing
  - 112 x 50cm (44 x 20in) square of soft, light-weight, cotton/polyester mix, sew-in wadding/batting: I have used #279 80/20 cotton mix by Vlieseline®, which is protected nicely by linen, but you could use Thermolam (also by Vlieseline®) as an alternative if you're cooking or usage is more nuclear
- Simple print stamps: I have used a small cactus to use for the back and front panels, a larger cactus for the 'focal' print on the hand pocket, and a border stamp
- Stamping inks: I have used several colours to 'colour' in different sections of my cacti
- 10mm (⅜in) brass Chicago screw, plus flat head screwdriver
- Awl (or see 'Optional')
- Your essential sewing kit (see page 11), plus walking foot
- Optional: revolving leather-punch pliers, bias tape maker

3 With the remaining fabric, cut out one 17 x 22cm (6¾ x 8½in) rectangle. Use this to help you cut out a slightly larger rectangle from the same fabric. These will be the main front and back pieces for your pot holder. Using a similar technique to the one above, print the right sides of the rectangles with your smaller stamp design – here, I am using the smaller cactus and making an all-over print.

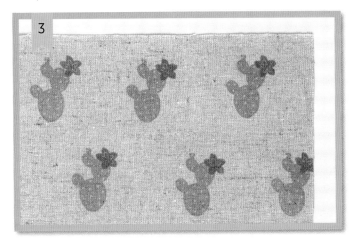

4 Once dry, press all the printed fabrics. Cut a piece of wadding/batting to the size of the hand pocket backing piece. Lay the backing fabric on a surface, right side facing down, then place the wadding/batting piece on top. Take the hand pocket square with the central motif and centre it on top of both layers to finish your quilt sandwich. Pin.

TIP

I prefer to pin from the centre outwards in each direction, smoothing all layers as I go so that I know they are as level as possible for quilting. On a small make like this pot holder, or the mug rug on pages 78–83, it is not such an issue. But it is a skill that's good to learn in preparation for future, bigger projects.

5 Now for our tribute to Chanel! For ease, I am demonstrating the quilting on a plain, non-printed quilt sandwich. Set up your machine with a walking foot. At a 45-degree angle, quilt straight lines across the whole of your quilt sandwich, leaving a 2.5cm (1in) gap in between each line (top). Rotate your quilt sandwich by 90 degrees then repeat the process, allowing your second set of lines to intersect with the first and create the diamond pattern. Trim the wadding/batting and backing to the size of your top panel, and then round off the two bottom corners only with scissors.

6 Make a quilt sandwich with your main front and back pieces (here, the all-over, smaller cacti pattern): lay your back piece right side facing down, then lay a slightly smaller piece of wadding/batting on top, followed by your pot holder front with its right side facing up. Quilt in the same way as you did in Step 5.

7 Trim the layers to the size of the pot holder front, then round off all four corners. Take your bias binding and sew it along the top, straight edge of the hand pocket quilt sandwich. (See page 57 if you need reminding on how to apply bias binding.)

8 Lay the hand pocket over the top of the main pot holder quilt sandwich, lining up the hand pocket's rounded bottom edge with the rounded bottom edge of the main pot holder. Tack/baste the pocket to the main pot holder to secure temporarily.

9 Bind the whole perimeter of the pot holder. This will secure all the layers together.

10 Trim the leather scrap to 12.5 x 2cm (5 x ¾in), fold in half and punch a hole through each end using an awl (or revolving leather-punch pliers). Punch a hole in the top left-hand corner of the pot holder too. Sandwich the pot holder between the folded leather end and insert the Chicago screw, taking care to line up all of the holes as accurately as you can.

KEEPING YOUR SANDWICH TOGETHER PRIOR TO QUILTING

We have talked about pinning the quilt sandwich layers so that movement is restricted. The last thing that you want is for your layers to shift (and they will thanks to our ol' buddy friction). This means that you can finish the make, only to find that the back panel and interfacing have slipped and you have a section of top fabric with nothing underneath it. This means unpicking. And. Starting. Again. This fabric shift is even harder to spot early on with a large make like a bed quilt. Of course, the answer is to either pin or spray tack/baste to keep the layers together. Personally, I am not a fan of spray tacking/basting. For one thing, pins can be repositioned easily. I use 'normal' sewing pins for a small make and special quilting safety pins for a quilt. The latter don't come out so easily, and are longer too – ideal for multiple layers of fabric.

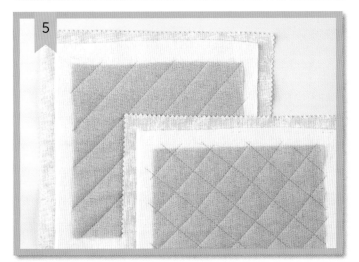

5

Hexie Pillow

One of the oldest forms of quilting is **English paper piecing** (known also as **EPP**). Traditionally, this is a sit-by-the-fire sort of patchwork that doesn't need a sewing machine, making it a bit more portable.

Basically, you decide on a pattern shape – hexagons, or **'hexies'** to the avid quilter, are a bit of a classic – then you cut this pattern shape out of paper. The next step is to cover the paper with fabric; this is the same shape as the paper, just a little bigger to allow you to wrap it around the paper shape, that you then tack/baste in place. Keep doing this to make as many shapes as you need. Then, to finish, you hand-stitch these fabric-covered shapes together as invisibly as possible to make a kaleidoscopic surface pattern! The paper in each shape is then removed and this pieced top interfaced, backed and quilted in the same way as the pot holder (see Step 5, page 91).

It is a lovely old-fashioned method with an old-fashioned feel, but it is a slow process. For this pillow cover we're going to modernize the method to give your EPP a totally different feel (and make the process a little quicker too!). Let's take a look below.

SEWING 101

A new (and quicker) way of EPP

Normally when making an item with the EPP method, you do not remove the papers until each shape is fully surrounded by others. This is to help it to keep its shape. With the method that I am going to show you, the papers can be removed earlier because your shape won't be joined to any others, and will stand alone. To secure the shape of the fabric and set the creases, press it first then allow it to cool. Then snip or unpick the tacking/basting thread and carefully remove the paper. Gently fold the fabric edges back in.

So if we're not sewing the shapes together, how do we EPP? Here's the next unusual bit: we're going to treat our shapes as appliqué, tacking/basting them in place onto our base fabric then machine quilting them in place to secure. Not only does this method give you the opportunity to play around with the layout and design of your EPP pillow cover, it's much quicker than sewing each paper piece together by hand.

Choosing your paper for paper piecing

For obvious reasons, paper plays an important part in EPP. Pundits will assure you that you must not use cheap stuff like old catalogues and magazines; you must buy special EPP papers.

Erm. This is not my experience, actually, and I have made a lot of quilts with junk mail. You can, of course, buy the pattern papers – and they will be more accurate, especially if you need hundreds to make a quilt – but for smaller items like this, tearing up old paper and 'zines for cutting is fine. The only thing that I would avoid is newspaper because the print can rub off – although I'll bet that this is what the pioneer women would have used if that was all they had!

If you have a die-cutting machine, think about die-cutting the paper shapes too – this makes the cutting process quicker as they can cut a fair few in minutes. Hexie dies tend to come in a small range of sizes.

Choose your weapon... the different ways of cutting your paper pieces. From left to right: magazine, wrapping paper, special EPP paper, die-cutter.

Making a pillow cover

For me, the worst thing about a handmade pillow is making one that's too floppy. I like to make the outer case quite firm, so besides interfacing both the front and back pillow pieces, I like to quilt over the back pieces too. Interfacing the cover completely adds rigidity, but quilting the back (in addition to the front) 'magically' adds more structure to the fabric too and makes it tighter. This back piece is usually one large piece of fabric, so I use the wholecloth quilting technique and sew the same quilting pattern on the back as the one used on the front.

PATTERN

1 For this pillow, we'll be using the traditional hexie shape and making eighteen hexies to appliqué onto the pillow front. To begin, prepare your hexie shape using either a bought EPP hexie, a die-cut one, or one transferred from Pattern Sheet A. Pin your hexie to the wrong side of your floral FQ or a floral scrap and trim the fabric to the shape of your hexie, making sure you leave a 2cm (¾in) seam allowance all around your paper piece.

2 Fold one edge over, then the next and so on, finger pressing each time to crease. Tack/baste the the edges in place temporarily by hand.

3 Press your hexie with an iron and leave to cool. Unpick one stitch with a quick unpick.

4 Carefully remove your paper piece and fold any bent edges back in place. You should have a perfect fabric hexagon ready to appliqué! Repeat Steps 1–4 with the remaining seventeen hexies.

GATHER THESE SUPPLIES:

◎ Fabric
  - FQ of neutral quilting cotton, for the pillow front
  - FQ (or scraps) of floral quilting cotton, for EPP
  - FQ of corresponding patterned quilting cotton, for the pillow back

◎ Interfacing
  - Two 56cm (22in) squares of soft, light-weight, cotton/polyester mix, sew-in wadding/batting: I have used #279 80/20 cotton mix by Vlieseline®

◎ 50cm (20in) square pillow pad

◎ Paper, for making the paper pieces

◎ Your essential sewing kit (see page 11), plus walking foot

TEMPLATE ON PATTERN SHEET A

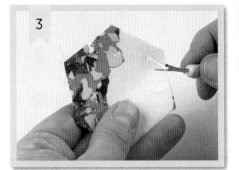

SAVING PAPER

One advantage to this method is that you could actually use the same hexie template to prepare all your fabric hexies – saving more effort, money and paper! If you decide to do this, I recommend using a slightly tougher template material – such as card – to make it a little more long-lasting.

STORING SCRAPS

If you like these hexie patterns, consider making a few every time you have suitable scraps. As I mentioned earlier (and often) never throw your scraps away. Consider cutting up your scraps as above or in useful strips for patching and arrange them by colour or size in bags or boxes. Storing scraps this way has a two-fold benefit: not only does it make your collection much nicer and easier to root through – as opposed to facing a threatening mound of disparate fabrics squashed in the corner of your room – but you also have some ready-to-go quilting components so that, if the muse descends, you can get on with the making.

5 Trim your FQ of neutral fabric to a 50cm (20in) square and lay out your hexies in a pleasing way. Once you are happy with the arrangement, dab a bit of fabric glue on the back of each one to keep it in place temporarily. For my pillow, I made a ring of six hexies at the centre of the fabric, then surrounded them with another ring with the remaining hexies, leaving a 1cm (⅜in) gap in between each one.

TIP

I have chosen to make a giant hexie motif but you can play around and make any shape that you like – you could even cover the whole pillow front with appliqué hexies! You may need to make some more though, if you decide to make a more complex design.

6 Lay your embellished pillow front fabric centrally onto one of the pieces of wadding/batting, right side facing up, then pin.

7 Set up your machine with a walking foot, then quilt the whole pillow front. You want to quilt though all the 'points' of the hexies. I recommend using the step photo below and the photo of the pillow, right, as a guide.

Starting with the bottom row of hexies, quilt a horizontal line that runs just underneath the base of the hexies, sew another through the middle of the hexies, and then sew another line just above the top of the hexies. Repeat this across the whole of the pillow, working from edge to edge. Sew additional 'rows' below and above the ring of hexies onto just the neutral fabric, to keep the quilting pattern consistent.

Now, sew diagonal lines across the whole of the front to stitch through the remaining 'points' on your hexies. Remember, each hexie should have a 'star' of quilting lines in the centre. You should end up with rows of little quilted triangles throughout the whole pillow front.

7

TIP

If the thought of quilting all these lines makes your nervous, use a quilting guide for your machine or draw them on first with a water-soluble marker pen and a quilting ruler. Then, just spritz your fabric with water when you've finished sewing to remove your guide lines.

8 Trim the wadding/batting back to the size of your pillow front. If your hexies form a central motif, like mine, make sure you trim all the edges of your pillow evenly to keep the design centred.

9 Lay the FQ backing fabric onto the remaining piece of wadding/batting, and quilt it using any of your favourite designs – I worked simple, diagonal lines (see the blue backed pillow, opposite). Don't trim it just yet.

10 Place the trimmed pillow front onto the untrimmed back, right sides facing. Sew around the perimeter using a normal seam allowance, leaving a turning gap in the bottom seam. Trim the backing up to the seam allowance and clip across the corners.

11 Turn out through the gap and insert the pillow pad. Close the gap by hand with ladder stitch. The pillow pad will fit snugly, giving a lovely plump look.

We have looked at Quilt As You Go (QAYG) already, when we made a pair of slippers (see pages 52–57), so you will be an old hand at this! In fact, the QAYG technique for this make is made exactly the same way as the slippers. The difference between this project and the slippers is that we will make the pattern from scratch! Don't worry, it is not at all difficult – I'll go through the technique with you in detail.

This project is an exciting one, and it's not only very useful but is another way of using up your scraps. I also have a really nice method of making a professional flap, which I'll share with you in detail very soon.

WHAT YOU WILL LEARN:

◎ QAYG: round two
◎ Drafting your own pattern
◎ How to make a professional flap

SEWING 101

Drafting your own pattern

We're making a tablet case here, but if you don't own a tablet the same principles below can be used to fit and make a sleeve for a portable games console or a sketchbook.

Using a pen and a piece of paper that is larger all around than your tablet, we're going to draw around the tablet to create the main shape of the tablet sleeve. However, if we cut out this drawn outline twice (to make the back and front of the sleeve) and sew them together, the tablet will not fit. So, we need to add an extra 1cm (⅜in) to the outline all the way around for our seam allowance, and then another 1cm (⅜in) for **ease**, to get the tablet in and out – overall, approximately an extra 2cm (¾in) all the way around is added to your outline to help your item fit in your sewn shape. Next, grab something round and round off the bottom two corners. A teacup usually works well for this.

Now what about the flap? Begin with a rectangle. This is to be as wide as the top edge (the edge without the rounded corners) and half the height of the main case. All round, draw in the seam allowance – as ease isn't as important here, we can use a regular 5mm (¼in) seam. Back to the crockery cupboard, and get out a slightly bigger cup or saucer. Round the two lower corners of the rectangle to finish the flap. That's it – you have drafted a pattern! The lining for the flap will be a rectangle the same size as you have made, plus an extra 2.5cm (1in) all around and left unrounded. We'll have our extra fabric here because, as you'll remember from earlier (if not, see the technique box on page 64), the lining fabric is almost never cut to size. All fabric shifts thanks to friction, and if the two pieces – plus their respective interfacing – are cut exactly to size, the layers are likely to move around and go off kilter as you sew, meaning you'll not catch all the layers and you'll need to start again. For this reason, it is much easier to leave the lining untrimmed and give yourself that additional 2.5cm (1in). You can then sew to your heart's content then trim down the lining, knowing you will be 100 per cent accurate. The lining to put inside the tablet will be the same size and shape as the main outer, which means the seam allowances are already calculated. Easy.

Naturally, not all patterns are so straightforward as this, but pattern-making is a useful skill to have and it might inspire you to find out more about drafting. I recommend using pattern paper if you can, as it includes little 5mm (¼in) squares within larger 2.5cm (1in) squares, making it easier for you to draw out your patterns more accurately. Otherwise, gift-wrapping paper with squares printed on the back makes a great, economical alternative.

How to make a professional flap

Now for my never-fail tip for making the most professional flap ever. The secret is the recipe of interfacing layers.

As you know, I really don't go for floppy bits anywhere that are not professional looking. A flap on a bag is a case in point. You might be tempted to leave the interfacing out because it is only a small thing. Don't even consider it! The flap must feel substantial (the devil is in the detail, remember?) and the only way for that to happen is to have not one layer, or even two, but THREE layers of interfacing! I kid you not. Nope, your eyes are not playing up and this is not a misprint. THREE layers. You will have the outer fabric and the lining, and in between these will be two layers of a light fusible wadding (H630) and a layer of non-woven (Decovil I Light) for structure.

As the Decovil I Light has no padding (but is needed to add that level of structure to the flap) you need the wadding/ batting in there to give it some much needed bulk. The finished result will be something that you keep touching to test that it is real – I really love this combination! I'll go into details on how to fuse all three layers together in the pattern.

LINGO: 'EASE'

Ease is about making sure your sewn-together fabric isn't so tight that it will tear before it moves (something that my sixteen-year-old self did not understand about jeans...). You do not want the case so tight that it measures the same dimensions as the tablet, as it will strain the seams. Adding ease will give the tablet a bit of wiggle room so that it can go in and out more easily.

PATTERN

What do you think? As you may have gathered, this sleeve is going to feel luxurious and substantial. Well, gather up that pattern and let's make the whole thing!

1 Draw around the tablet, onto the paper, then add 2cm (¾in) all round. Round off the bottom two corners. This is your main tablet pattern, that you will also use for the tablet lining. Draw the flap pattern separately: sketch a rectangle the same width as the tablet, about half of its overall height. My flap is 12.75cm (5in) high, based on a 25.5cm (10in) tablet. Add 5mm (¼in) all the way around for the seam allowance. Draw out an extra lining pattern for the flap: use the same rectangle you drew for the outer flap, then add 2.5cm (1in) all the way round. Cut out your paper patterns.

2 Take your tablet pattern and trace it twice onto the #279 80/20 cotton mix wadding/batting with a water-soluble marker pen. Remember that the idea is now to 'colour in' these outlines with your chosen scraps. Remember to lay the first scrap piece right side up then quilt over the top to secure; the rest of the strips will be laid right side down on top of the previous quilted strip, raw edges matching.

   Set up your machine with the walking foot. Sew the right-or left-hand side seams, flip the stitched strip over then quilt the same pattern used for the first strip over the top. (See also Steps 5 and 6 on pages 55–56 of the Spa Slippers project, if you would like to remind yourself how to do this.) Repeat across the whole of the two outer tablet panels.

3 Cut out your quilted outer tablet panels, trimming away any overhanging scrap edges (you may need to re-draw your tablet outline over the top beforehand, to ensure the outer tablet panels are cut out accurately).

4 Fold your lining fabric in half and pin your main tablet pattern to the lining fabric, lining it up with the selvedge/selvage of the fabric. Cut out two lining pieces.

GATHER THESE SUPPLIES:

- Fabric
  - Scraps of quilting cotton in one or several colours: you need enough to cover the front and the back of the case, so use your paper pattern to work it out
  - F8th of denim-style quilting cotton, for the flap
  - F8th of contrasting quilting cotton, for the lining
- Interfacing
  - 56cm (22in) square of soft, light-weight, cotton/polyester mix, sew-in wadding/batting: I have used #279 80/20 cotton mix by Vlieseline®
  - 45.75 x 28cm (18 x 11in) piece of light-weight, non-woven, fusible wadding/batting: I have used H630 by Vlieseline®
  - 45.75 x 28cm (18 x 11in) piece of light-weight, non-woven, fusible interlining: I have used Decovil I Light by Vlieseline®
  - 56cm (22in) square of flexible, light-weight, sew-in foam wadding/batting: I have used Style-Vil by Vlieseline®
- Awl (or see 'Optional')
- Snap fastener set plus snap pliers: I have used KAM snaps in size 20
- Two A3 (11¾ x 16½in) sheets of paper plus pencil, for drawing the tablet pattern: I have used graph paper
- Your essential sewing kit (see page 11), plus walking foot
- Optional: revolving leather-punch pliers

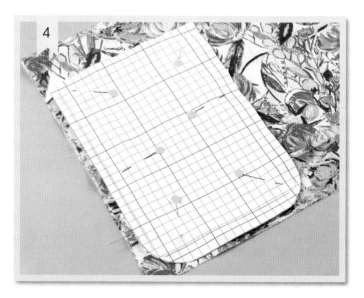

5 Use a narrow tacking/basting seam on your sewing machine (effectively a long top-stitch) to tack/baste one outer panel to the centre of a slightly larger piece of Style-Vil foam wadding/batting. Trim back the Style-Vil wadding/batting to the same size as the outer panel. Repeat with the other outer panel and another piece of Style-Vil.

6 With the right sides together, sew the sides and bottom edge of the outer tablet panels, then remove the tacking/basting stitches. Sew the two lining pieces together in the same way, this time leaving a turning gap in the short bottom seam of approx. 10cm (4in). Put it aside. Notch the curved corners of the outer panel, then turn it the right way out.

7 Take your flap template and trace it onto the denim fabric. Fuse the H630 to the wrong side. Leave to cool, then fuse the Decovil I Light on top. Leave to cool once more, then trim the two layers of interfacing to the size of the denim piece.
N.B.: To show you the layers of interfacing clearly, I have pulled back some of the fused Decovil I Light.

8 Draw your flap lining pattern onto the lining fabric and cut out, leaving approx. 2.5cm (1in) extra fabric all round and keeping the shape rectangular for now. Fuse the H630 to the wrong side of the flap lining. Pin the interfaced denim flap to the interfaced lining flap rectangle, right sides together. Sew around the sides and bottom of the flap, leaving the top straight edge open. Trim the interfaced flap lining down to the size of the denim flap and turn through the opening. Top-stitch around the seam, using a 5mm (¼in) seam allowance, to close the gap.

9 Punch a hole through the centre of the curve on the denim side of the flap, approx. 2cm (¾in) from the edge, and apply the male half of the snap fastener. Sew the bottom of the flap to the inside of the outer tablet sleeve, along the top back edge.

10 At the centre of the outer tablet front, measure 10cm (4in) down from the edge and punch a hole with an awl (or revolving leather-punch pliers). Install the female half of the snap fastener. Remember this measurement may vary if you are using a different-sized tablet, so fold the flap over the front first to check positioning before committing.

11 With the outer tablet sleeve the right way out and the lining inside out, stuff the outer inside the lining so right sides are together. Line up the top edges and side seams perfectly then pin in place. Sew right the way around the top edge, leaving no gaps and making sure the flap is out of the way. Turn the whole sleeve out through the gap in the lining then hand-sew the gap closed with ladder stitch. Stuff the lining down into the case and top-stitch along the top edge to keep the lining down.

TIP

This interfacing layering trick will make your project feel so much more professional. Note the difference between the outer panel with only the #279 80/20 wadding/batting, and the outer panel with the Style-Vil wadding/batting. Your tablet will thank you!

We are entering the rabbit hole now – the wonderful world of haberdashery! And what might that be? Haberdashery is the realm of small sewing items used mostly for embellishment, but it also includes fastenings to add more robust, adjustable and secure elements to your sewn items. This is, then, quite a broad group, from buttons, zips, bra clips and toggles through to hooks, eyelets and bag components. You have used them a fair bit already but now is the time for formal introductions...

Once the home sewist could only look wistfully at the finishing touches on professionally made items and wish that they could buy the tricksy components themselves. Fast forward a lot of years and we now have a haberdashery section in our world, the likes of which our grandparents could have only dreamed. These are the accessories that will elevate your makes (yes do forgive me for saying it again) from the dreaded 'homemade' to the one that we all want to hear – 'handmade'! While this first make isn't technically machine sewing, it'll segue us nicely into the later haberdashery projects that get a little more challenging.

While sewn items can be made without these accessories – and do feel free to have a think and come up with fabric alternatives – I fully recommend taking advantage of the choice of items out there. Your homework this week is to go looking. Fully explore what is available to you – either on the high/main street or online, and compare the looks that you might be able to achieve by, say, swapping a nylon zip for a metal one. And look at what can you put into the zipper pull – the range of ribbons around is jaw dropping! Have a look what you can 'borrow' from more unlikely sources too. I like looking at hardware stores for metal, chain and rope elements, and the world of jewellery making yields another treasure trove. Let's not forget all the new and fresh ideas for pompoms and tassels that have erupted over the last few years too. Happy hunting!

WHAT YOU WILL LEARN:

◎ Making a flower
◉ Haberdashery 101
◎ Attaching a brooch back
◎ Using fabric stiffener

SEWING 101

Making a flower

Let's make something this time that is very much sewing but not actually sewing... a flower! These are things you'll to learn how to sew, as they can decorate and coordinate with a wide variety of handmade items. If you are a milliner, they go onto hats; if you're a bag maker, think bag charms. They can become brooches and statement necklaces too. You can also sew them onto clothing, along a neckline, lapel or hem. Flowers are such perennial favourites, they are sure to be hit with whomever you make them for.

For this project, we're making a brooch-backed flower. You can die-cut the necessary flower shapes or find a flower outline and trace it onto paper to make a template. Or, mix and match and use both! (Of course, you can use the templates provided on Pattern Sheet B for ease.) I have made my flower from felt because I love its texture and look, but for summer-themed items or garments you could consider flowers made from layers of pretty cotton fabric. In fact, fabric stiffener would be perfect for cotton fabric flowers, to give their layers some body (see right for more details).

Attaching a brooch back

To make our flower, we will be borrowing the brooch setting from our jeweller friends. There are two types of brooch backs you can buy: sew-on and glue-on. It really is up to you which one you choose. I prefer the glue-on types, as they are less fiddly to use and, as long as you have the right glue (I like hot glue best), they will stay put. Before applying the glue, I also like to scratch the plate on which the flower will adhere with sandpaper. The scratching provides a 'key' or rough surface that gives the glue something to grab onto, helping it and the flower stick.

Using fabric stiffener

Another item usually found in the haberdashery section is fabric stiffener (which goes to show you how diverse this section can be!). This is used to saturate fabric, and when it dries it allows you to mould and hold the shape of whatever you are applying it to. The finish on the stiffener is rather like hair with hairspray on it. The reason I like to use this for projects like these is that I find fabric flowers can be a little bit sad and flat looking without any help; putting fabric stiffener on and then scrunching the flowers gives them more dimension and shape. It works on almost all fabrics, and with practice you will get the most amazing results.

PATTERN

Before we get to the pattern, there are so many ways to make a centre for your flower, but one of my favourites (again from the haberdashery section) is the pompom trim. This comes in a huge array of colours and for flowers like this, it is simply a matter of snipping off one of the pompoms and hot gluing it to the centre!

1 Using one of the methods described on page 101, cut out the flower components from felt – I cut two small flower heads, and two large ones.

1 Using one of the methods described on page 101, cut out the flower components from felt – I cut two small flower heads, and two large ones.

TIP

With felt, you will need only two of each flower head to create volume. However, with thinner fabric (like quilting cotton for example) the more layers you can use the better.

---

2 Paint the felt pieces with enough fabric stiffener on both sides to saturate them, then scrunch the felt to make a flower shape. Put them aside to dry. This can take a while; a warm window or airing cupboard will speed the process along.

GATHER THESE SUPPLIES:

- Fabric
  - Scraps of corresponding wool-blend felt, ideally in flower colours: as long as they fit the template, they are big enough! You need enough for two layers of each size
- Pompom trim, from which to cut the flower centre: centres are usually orange or yellow (to attract the bees) but do have a play – black looks awesome on a light coloured flower. Whatever you do, if the flower is darker, the centre looks better light and vice versa
- Fabric stiffener
- Brooch back, 20mm (¾in) in diameter
- Hot-glue gun and glue
- Sandpaper
- Your essential sewing kit (see page 11)
- Optional: manual die-cutting machine plus flower dies

TEMPLATES ON PATTERN SHEET B

3 When the flower petals are dry, assemble the flower by placing the two largest ones together with the petals offset (not exactly on top of one another with the petals in layers), followed by the smallest ones; these should be offset too. When you are happy with their placement, glue them together with a hot-glue gun and glue.

4 Scratch the adhering section of the brooch setting with sandpaper to give your glue a textured surface to grip onto. Glue the bottom of the flower to the setting and leave to dry.

5 Make the centre by snipping a pompom off the trim. Glue this to the centre and leave to dry. Your flower is finished!

TIP

As you only need one pompom per flower, it is a great way to use up end bits of old pompom trims that would have been difficult to use for anything else.

TIP

If you like trying out different crafts, consider making your own felt for this project. It is easy, fun and there is a lot of information online showing how to do it.

Tribal Bag Charm

This project is all about adornment, and making something simple yet very professional looking. Not everything about machine sewing has to be a major undertaking, and this is a lovely, simple, enjoyable project to make in a very short space of time. Its easiness will also show you how far you've come in your sewing journey! There is some specific hardware for this charm, and I'm going to show you another use for leather and felt; I'll also tell you a new way of making a tassel.

WHAT YOU WILL LEARN:

◉ Adding eyelets
◉ Attaching a swivel clip
◉ Making tassels
◉ Using and adding gold foil

SEWING 101

Adding eyelets

Right-o! Shall we start with the hardware? If you make a charm or anything that has to be attached to something else, you have the choice of making it permanent or removable. Permanent is pretty straightforward actually – just sew it on. However, I like the idea of making use of other pieces of bespoke hardware. My go-to in this case is the swivel clip or trigger clip (which I'll get onto in a moment), and to attach it we'll need to add an eyelet.

Why bother with an eyelet, you may cry; why not just make a hole and leave it at that? Well, you can do, but your make will look much more professional if the hole is lined with an eyelet. Furthermore, an eyelet will prevent the hole you make from tearing or wearing, which could lead to your charm falling out accidentally. Finally, knowing how to add an eyelet is quite useful: besides serving a practical purpose, they add a nice decorative effect to items – especially nautical-themed ones. In my opinion, anything vaguely nautical has to have them – it is almost a law!

Eyelets can be put on in a few ways. There are kits where you get some odd-looking tools (all explained on the packet though) and you'll need a hammer too. Or, you can get en eyelet setting tool which looks like an overgrown pair of pliers.

The bonus of the kits is that the tools inside come in all sizes and so will perfectly match any size eyelet you find. The downside is that you have to learn to hit the eyelets in a certain way or they will go wonky, and getting them off again can be a tedious job. The trick with these kits is to make sharp, determined hits with the hammer and make sure you hit the eyelets straight on. The setting tool is easier to use but only suits one size eyelet, so you will need to either buy that particular size eyelet or buy several setting tools. In addition there is an upper size limit to these tools, so some of the really big eyelets cannot be put in this way and will need a hammer.

Whew! That was a lot of proing and conning. My advice? Get a small kit and be prepared to waste all of the eyelets in it while you practise with a hammer – saying that, you might get it right first time! As long as you make a note of the size of the eyelet, you can just buy more of these from your hardware store.

Attaching a swivel clip

We'll be looking at another way of adding the swivel clip to an item in the next project (see pages 108–111); in this one, we're going to have the help of a split ring. But first, let's take a look at swivel clips themselves.

These guys get called a lot of names (trigger clips, swivel clasps, lanyard snap hooks, lobster clasps), so be aware of this when having a look for one online or in a craft store. As the name suggests, the clip swivels to allow the item attached to it to move around and rotate easily. You can get swivel clips in different colours too: there are the ones that you would expect, such as gold, silver and bronze, and then are more unusual ones – shiny black, gunmetal and most of the other colours in the rainbow. In fact, there are even patterned ones.

To create enough space between our eyelet and swivel clip, but ensure the clip is securely in place, we're using a split ring as a joining ring. All key rings use one as they are strong yet are easily opened to fasten on a swivel clip – and charm – securely.

Making tassels

Life would not be so fabulous without tassels! You can use them in so many applications, and the great news is that they are easy peasy to make.

A tassel can be made in many ways, but I like to use a lovely tool by Clover (get that wish list out again...). The reason I have gone with this option is that this tool is adjustable, and so allows you to make tassels in lots of different sizes. I won't go into a lot of detail here because it comes with great instructions.

Just about anything can be used to make a tassel – even really thin strips of fabric offcuts will work! (I was not exaggerating before when I said that there was not much waste from sewing!). My tassel material favourites are perle coton à broder, mercerized cotton yarn, regular cotton yarn and wool. For small tassels, stranded embroidery cotton works really well too. Basically, the larger and meatier the project, the larger the yarn that you can use. It is a great way to use offcuts and you can experiment with texture to your heart's content.

Using and adding gold foil

There are constant new additions to the world of sewing – the sort of things that would have caused our grandmothers to gasp with amazement. Gold foil is one of these, and I love this stuff. It comes in shiny, matt and glittery finishes, and you can get other foil colours too. In addition, foil die-cuts perfectly and looks super schmick and professional. You simply iron it onto your fabric, and I'll give details of this below. Only one caveat – promise me that you will use an ironing cloth when you apply it? Your iron will never forgive you if it touches the hot iron plate.

PATTERN

Well we are ready for the pattern now. This is the most fantastic use of scrappy bits and it goes to show that although craft things can feel a bit pricey, you really do get a lot of mileage.

1 Cut your leather feather first. If you're using the die-cut option, trim away the stem. Otherwise, use the template on Pattern Sheet B. Punch a hole in the top of the feather with an awl (or the revolving leather-punch pliers) and attach one of the split rings.

2 Use the other template to cut two main triangular shapes from the felt. Use the template again to cut out the chevron from the gold iron-on foil. Fuse the chevron to the centre of one felt triangle, then peel away the backing – don't forget your ironing cloth here!

GATHER THESE SUPPLIES:

- Fabric
  - 20cm (8in) square piece of thick wool-blend felt
  - 15 x 7cm (6 x 2¾in) piece of leather
- Perle coton à broder, in your favourite colour
- Medium bronze swivel clip
- Two medium bronze split rings
- Small bronze eyelet, plus the necessary tools
- Small piece of gold iron-on foil
- Clover tassel maker
- Awl (or see 'Optional')
- Your essential sewing kit (see page 11)
- Optional: revolving leather punch pliers, manual die-cutting machine plus feather die

TEMPLATES ON PATTERN SHEET B

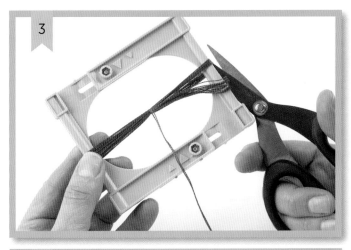

3 Grab your tassel maker and choose your tassel size. There are some triangular marks on the side and these have to be aligned correctly. For our tassel here, I am using the middle setting. Take the perle coton à broder and wrap this about twenty-five times around the tassel maker. Then take another length of perle coton à broder, approx. 25cm (10in) long and tie this around the centre. In the official maker instructions, it tells you to trim down this length and incorporate it in the tassel – don't do that this time. You need to keep this tie long, as you will use it to anchor and sandwich the tassel between the felt pieces later. Once you've tied off the centre, cut the loops on either side of the knot to free the tassel from the maker.

4 Fold the tassel over and keep the tie at the top. Cut off another length of perle coton à broder and tie the centre off to secure the fold, about 1cm (³⁄₈in) down from the top. Repeat Steps 3 and 4 to make two more tassels.

5 Lay all your tassels centrally at the bottom of one felt piece, with the extra lengths of perle coton à broder at the top of the tassels laid in the middle of the felt triangle, as shown.

6 When you are happy with the positioning of your tassels, glue them in place with fabric glue. Glue the felt piece on top of them, sandwiching the top tassel lengths and temporarily securing it all together before sewing. Machine sew around the edge of the triangle, and around the edge of the gold chevron shape.

7 Punch a hole at the top of your tasselled triangles the same size as your eyelet, using an awl (or revolving leather-punch pliers). Put the eyelet in and then take the little washer and put that on the back – the purpose of the washer is to give an anchor point that the back of the eyelet will curl around. Use your preferred eyelet setting method to set the eyelet.

8 Attach the second split ring to the swivel clip, then thread this through the eyelet in the tasselled triangle. Attach the feather to the bottom of the swivel clip too, using its split ring.

COTTON WEBBING & D-RING SWIVEL CLIPS

Camera Strap

One of the most exciting things in a haberdashery section for me are the bag-making components, so let's talk about hardware for bags (and other things). Don't overlook the potential this make has: although it is designed to be a camera strap, you could easily use it as a bag strap too. Things like these – handles and straps – are easy to mix and match in bag making, so the concept will not go to waste.

We have already made the acquaintance of the swivel clip, so no need to dwell there. However, we will be stepping up and using one with a D-ring – another cool piece of hardware – and we'll be cutting out our leather piece in a certain way this time, to help us attach the D-ring swivel clip to our main camera strap material – the cotton webbing. Let's have a look at all of these in more detail.

WHAT YOU WILL LEARN:
◉ Swivel clips with D-rings
◉ Dressing up cotton webbing
◉ Making a leather casing for your strap

SEWING 101

Swivel clips with D-rings

Swivel clips with D-rings fall into that category of things that will help to make your project look more professional. They are available anywhere where bag-making things are for sale and, like regular swivel clips, can come in a few sizes and colours. You can use swivel clips for bags, for straps (as you see here) and for keyrings, dog leads and accessories. The best feature of them (apart from the swivel bit which ensures that the strap doesn't twist and stay that way) are the clips, which mean that you are not committed to having the strap and can detach it. Oh the possibilities!

Dressing up cotton webbing

Before we get to the project, another great find in the haberdashery section is cotton webbing. This is perfect for bag handles as it's nice and strong. I definitely recommend buying cotton webbing in all colours to make bag handles, straps and – if you're delving into the world of dressmaking in the future – belts too.

Saying that, it can be a bit boring by itself so a great way to dress it up is to add a strip of fabric or straight binding down the centre. Have a look at your fabric and see which will suit your colour webbing. Then, cut out your strip of fabric to the same width as the webbing that you want to cover, cutting it on the straight grain. Remember, you can work out the straight grain of your fabric usually from the selvedge/selvage edge of the fabric. You then fold over the raw edges of the strip for the seam allowances, and then attach the strip to the webbing – I'll go into more detail about how to do this in the main pattern overleaf.

Making a leather casing for your strap

Finally, you get to make some bespoke leather strap ends too. It is easy peasy to do, and my big tip for this is to cut yourself out a template from stiffer material, such as cardboard, to make it easier to draw around (keep it in case you want to make more too).

You will see that there is some top-stitching on the leather and this gives your strap a cool retro look (we could stop here). However, it also has a functional purpose in that it is STRONG! This stitching will ensure your webbing and swivel clips are not going anywhere! Pretty important when you consider that your camera is dangling in space from the end of it....

Do have a look around for leather thread (Gütermann have some fab ones in great colours) and a leather needle for your machine. Leather needles do not cut the leather the way a fabric sewing needle can. They are not expensive and you get a few in the pack. Other than that, go slow and sew deliberately to get the stitching perfect, and reverse stitch each time you start or finish to prevent unravelling.

PATTERN

Let's get ready to go! When you choose the size of the D-ring swivel clips for your camera, pay attention to the size of the tabs on either side of your camera. The hooks on the swivel clips need to fit through them. If the camera tabs are quite small, you can attach split rings to give your swivel clips something to hang onto.

1 Begin by trimming the cotton webbing ends neatly to remove any stray threads.

TIP

Once they have been trimmed, it doesn't hurt to coat the ends of the cotton webbing with fray stopper, to prevent further fraying.

2 Take your strip of patterned fabric and fold the raw edges under by 5mm (¼in) on each side, wrong sides together. Press.

3 Lay this strip centrally over the webbing strap then hold it in place with double-sided tape, sticking this along the middle of the fabric strip on the wrong side. Sew narrowly along both long sides of the fabric strip, using coordinating thread.

TIP

Make sure you keep the taped section of the fabric strip away from the needle! The glue on it will gum up your needle and, even though you can wipe it, there will still be some residue that could cause missed stitches while sewing along with other infuriating problems. Choose the narrowest tape you can find and make sure it is placed at the centre of the fabric strip only.

GATHER THESE SUPPLIES:

- Fabric
  - 4 x 85cm (1½ x 33½in) strip of patterned fabric, to coordinate with your colour webbing
  - 15cm (6in) square piece of tan leather
- 85cm (33½in) length of 4cm (1½in) wide cotton webbing
- Double-sided sticky tape
- Two silver swivel clips with D-rings, 2.5cm (1in) wide
- Your essential sewing kit (see page 11)
- Optional: decorative ribbon, fray stopper

TEMPLATE ON PATTERN SHEET B

WHY NOT PIN OR GLUE WEBBING?

You can pin or glue your fabric to your webbing if you wish, but I prefer and recommend using double-sided tape for temporarily tacking/basting. Pins can distort when pushed through such thick material, and because of the highly absorbent nature of webbing, glue is likely to soak in and unlikely to hold the fabric in place.

4 Using the tab template, transfer and cut out two tabs from the square of leather. Top-stitch the middle bits of both tabs, as shown. This means that when you sew the tab on, it looks as though it is sewn all the way around, but without the clunky effect of doubled-up stitching.

5 Take one tab and apply glue to one end, on the wrong side of the leather. Stick it to one end of the webbing strap, at the back. Slide the D-ring swivel clip over the free end of the tab. Apply glue to the wrong side of this end, then fold it over to cover the front of the webbing. Top-stitch through both the layers: stitch a box first, then sew a cross inside it to finish.

TIP

You will have greater success top-stitching your leather tab if you use a leather needle.

6 Repeat for the other end of the webbing strap with the remaining tab.

7 If you wish, finish off your strap by cutting up some decorative ribbon and gluing it at one end – I used a Union Jack print ribbon. Clip your strap end to your camera tabs and get snapping!

Travel Keepsake Bag

Okay, we have put this off long enough – it is time to install a zip!

Seriously, don't panic about it though. I have a small hypothesis which may go a long way to explaining why people are so scared of zips. Remember how I touched on before that my Nana taught me on an old Singer treadle machine that had only one presser foot? That presser foot had to do everything, so there were some things it did quite badly, one of these being attaching zips – they were a nightmare. And, unfortunately, that nightmare stuck with me and created a real fear that my modern machines years later had to dispel. But, you'll be happy to hear, my new sewing machines HAVE dispelled it, and it turns out that the answer is simply using the right tool for the right job.

WHAT YOU WILL LEARN:

◎ What's special about a zip foot?
◎ Plastic vs. metal zips
◎ Shortening a plastic zip
◎ Installing a zip 101

SEWING 101

What's special about a zip foot?

All modern machines (should) come with a zip foot. Find yours and see how it fits together (the manual that comes with your sewing machine will help you with this). This foot allows you to sew close to your zip, thanks to its shape (notice the indentations on the left and right sides? The needle passes through there, so you can sew really close to the zip teeth. It is great for putting on binding too, especially if the bound edges of your items are bulky, such as the binding for quilts.

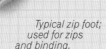

Typical zip foot; used for zips and binding.

Plastic vs. metal zips

The make for this chapter is a travel keepsake bag and it has a plastic zip. So what is the difference between using plastic and metal for zips? I tend to opt for metal ones most of the time because they are stronger, look a little edgier and, for some reason, I feel that it makes a bag look more professional. However, plastic zips have their place too. They are easier to shorten for a start (more on that in a bit) and plastic zips come in all the colours of the rainbow. You can also get super-long plastic zips for things like sleeping bags, open-ended ones for jackets and heavy-duty ones for items that require stronger zips. When I am making a bag, I will often use metal ones on the outside and plastic ones for pockets in the lining. This is because plastic zips are not going to scratch things – your phone, for example. That is also why this make has a plastic zip: it is intended to house my stockings one day, so a little kindness is required.

Shortening a plastic zip

First question I bet you're asking is 'Why bother? Just buy the right length?' Well, yes, I see your point but there are a few good reasons why you may wish to shorten a zip. Besides the common practical issues – it is 10pm on a Saturday night and you want to finish a project, and you have the perfect coloured zip but it is too long – one reason is that it is easier to work with a slightly longer zip and shorten it afterwards: to sew on a zip you need to move the zipper pull out of the way, and sewing on a zip that's longer than the project allows you to do this without awkwardly moving the zipper pull up and down as you're sewing the main tape in place. If you are using heavy-duty plastic zips you'll likely need to trim these too, as they tend to be open ended. On a bag, a heavier zip looks amazing but you don't want or need it open ended; so, removing the bit on the end without actually shortening the zip solves the problem.

Whatever the case, it is easy to shorten a plastic zip. I'll show you how to do this shortly.

Installing a zip 101

So okay, how do we put it in? First of all, you'll need to lay out your zip along the intended opening and tack/baste it in place. Tacking/basting keeps the zip stable enough for sewing. If you are lining your item (as we will here), this is the point when you will need to lay your lining fabric on top of the zip to make a **zip sandwich**. Finally, set up your machine and sew it in place – simple! As your zip will be slightly too long, you'll need to trim it down to size – this is easy to do, now the zip is secure. Sew across the 'open' end of the two tapes; this effectively makes a new stopper for the zip. You don't need to do a lot of stitching, nor does it need to be very neat or even in the same colour as the zip, because it will be hidden. The extra can then be merrily snipped off. Don't worry if this all sounds confusing; I'll provide a little more detail in the pattern overleaf.

PATTERN

1 Make an 80cm (31½in) length of bias binding with your FQ of fabric (see Steps 7–9 on page 87, if you'd like to remind yourself of how to make your own bias tape).

2 From the FQ of floral fabric, cut one 23cm (9in) square piece for the bag front and one 33 x 23cm (13 x 9in) piece for the bag back. Fuse the H630 to the wrong side of each and trim to size.

3 To make a decorative label for the front of your bag, cut out your desired leather shape and stamp on your chosen design. Glue the stamped leather shape to the front piece on the right side, approx. 5cm (2in) down from the top edge, then sew it in place. (See page 34, Steps 2 and 3 for more details.)

GATHER THESE SUPPLIES:

- ◎ Fabric
  - FQ of floral quilting cotton, for the outer
  - FQ of coordinating quilting cotton, for the lining
  - FQ of contrasting quilting cotton, for the bias binding: I'm using diagonal striped fabric
  - Scrap of leather, to decorate the front and zipper pull
- ◎ Interfacing
  - 56cm (22in) square of light-weight, non-woven, fusible wadding/batting: I have used H630 by Vlieseline®
- ◎ 30.5cm (12in) plastic zip, to coordinate with your fabric
- ◎ Ink pad plus stamp of your choice, for the decorative label on the front
- ◎ 30.5cm (12in) length of perle coton à broder, to decorate the zip pull
- ◎ Your essential sewing kit (see page 11), plus zip foot
- ◎ Optional: bias tape maker, ribbon

4 Find something round like a dinner plate (about 23cm/9in in diameter) and round off the bottom edges of the front and back bag pieces. Use the outer pieces as a template to cut out corresponding lining pieces.

5 Lay the zip onto the right side of the bag front, the zipper pull facing down and one long side of the zip tape matching the top raw edge of the fabric. Ensure one end of the zip tape, ideally the one allowing you to close the zip when you pull the zipper pull out of the way, is aligned with one side of the bag front. Tack/baste this top long side only. Once the tacking/basting stitches are in place, you can pull the zipper pull out of the way, towards the stopper. Lay the corresponding square lining piece on top, right side facing down and matching its raw edge with the zip tape and bag front's raw edge. Tack/baste the lining in place along this edge, this time closer to the zip teeth. This is your zip sandwich! Sew along the zip using a normal seam allowance, then remove your tacking/basting stitches.

TIP

You could pin these layers together if you wish, but I prefer to tack/baste (either by hand or machine) at this stage because pins distort the fabrics and they get in the way. Tacking/basting holds everything nice and steady. And, if you use a very narrow seam, you won't even have to remove the tacking/basting stitches.

6 Flip all the layers over so the sewn zip tape is sandwiched between the lining and bag front, and the front panel is facing up. Press the fabric along the tape edge, then top-stitch all along the zip tape to finish off this side of the zip neatly.

7 Now for the other side! Attach the remaining outer and lining pieces to the other side of the zip, as in Steps 5 and 6.

8 Now your zip is secure, you can trim back the longer end. Mark the necessary length needed with a water-soluble marker pen. Sew across the tapes to create a new stopper. Cut off the unwanted end of the zip, leaving 1cm (⅜in) extra or so for fabric shift.

9 Open the zip about halfway. Fold over the fabric pieces, lining sides facing, and align the curved bottom edges of the front and back. Pin then tack/baste together all around.

10 Attach the bias binding around the sides and bottom of the bag. (See Steps 10 and 11 on page 57 if you would like help with this.)

11 Cut a long, thin strip from the remaining leather. Slide this through the hole in the zipper pull and then fold one end over the other, wrong sides together. Wrap the length of perle coton à broder around the top – a little bit like you're making a tassel – then glue in place to secure.

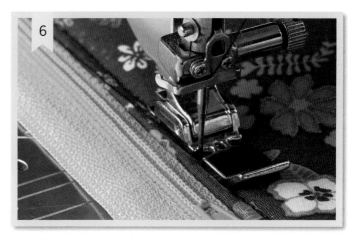

Top-stitching the zip tape. See how the needle can get nice and close to the zip? This is much trickier with a regular presser foot.

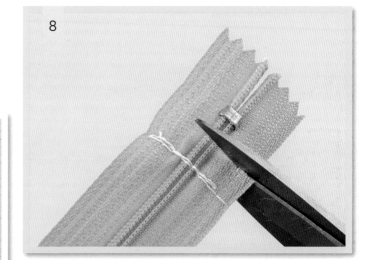

DECORATING YOUR ZIPPER PULL

I don't like to leave my zipper pull undecorated; it seems unfinished somehow. There are lots of ways that you can decorate them; some of my favourites include ribbon, baker's twine, thin leather scraps, charms, tassels and pompoms. Have a play and come up with something fab!

If you choose ribbon, don't forget to treat the end with fray stopper. This is a quick-drying solution in a bottle, and when painted onto the ends of the ribbon will stop the edges from fraying and unravelling.

#selfie Make-Up Pouch

By now you will see that putting in a zip is not a death warrant; it just requires a little extra preparation and confidence!

Well, I would be very remiss if I left you alone without sharing another little zip trick. There are as many ways of putting in zips as there are days in the week, and not all of them work every time. This can be very frustrating – when something is hit and miss and you are not sure why, it is impossible to avoid the misses and get it right every time, or even at all.

This method is different, and uses binding for the ends of the zip. The zip is also not actually part of the bag outer or lining but nestles perfectly in between, so that nothing can fall out. It is one of my most important technique discoveries and I use it constantly, so I thought that it was time to pass it on!

The other thing that I want to talk about in this chapter is how to get a nice, two-coloured fabric effect without fiddling around with seam allowances and 12,650,376 pattern pieces. Let's check out the basics below.

WHAT YOU WILL LEARN:

◎ THE best way of putting a top zip on a pouch

◎ How to make a fuss-free, two-coloured pouch

◎ Inserting darts

SEWING 101

THE best way of putting a top zip on a pouch

Let's get that zip out of the way first! And, while we're at it, I think we should give the metal zips an airing this time too. We're going to trim back our zip tape and tack/baste the ends as per the previous pattern. However, this is not only to make the zip the perfect size for our pouch but it will also allow the pieces of straight binding (remember this guy?) to fit exactly on each end and come up to the edge of the zip stop. You'll be encasing each end of the zip with the straight binding, folding it lengthways with the raw edges inside and then trimming to size once you've glued it in place. 'Glue?', I hear you cry? I kid you not. I used to sew and top-stitch these ends on and my machine did not like it one bit! I broke a needle too because I misjudged the amount of space that I had. Then I realized that you do not need to sew. The zip binding is really narrow and it will be sewn on either side anyway when you attach the lining and the outer. So glue the binding on each end and clip it in place until it dries. Once this is done, we're going to sandwich this bound-end zip in between the outer and lining fabrics, just as we did in the previous project.

You can use this method anywhere you have to install a top zip and it is the most liberating thing! Not so tricky after all, right?

How to make a fuss-free, two-coloured pouch

You will see in the main photo that there is a contrasting bit of fabric on the bottom of the pouch. This is very easily done. Have a look at your template (see Pattern Sheet A) – notice the dividing line? Keep this in mind because we will need it in a second.

Cut a piece of fabric for the top and a piece for the bottom then sew them together; the bigger bit is on top. Follow the pattern instructions to fuse or attach interfacing to the back – as you're treating these two joined pieces as one panel, you simply cut out the interfacing to the size of the whole joined piece. Grab your template and lay it on top, lining up the dividing line on the template with the fabric join. Pin and cut out your intended shape. I did say that it was easy!

Some patterns require two separate templates to achieve the same effect, and that is more fiddly. You can use this method for that sort of pattern too; simply be more generous with how much fabric you cut out, to accommodate seam allowances and potential fabric shift.

Inserting darts

Another detail that this bag has is **darts**. Odd term, I know. If you're not familiar with it, this a sewing technique that involves cutting out or pinching a triangle in the fabric, to take in the fabric slightly, and give more shape to the item in question. It's more often associated with dressmaking, where you need to shape a garment in a way to fit the contours of the body; however, darts works very well with accessories too, as you can create professional, softly curved shapes. Darts are not difficult to make, plus you feel so grown up sewing them!

How you prepare the darts varies from pattern to pattern. Some will ask you to draw out the triangles on the fabric, others will ask you to cut out the triangles. I like to cut them out as this creates less bulk in the fabric, and we don't need to worry about ease or 'letting out' the fabric as you would in dressmaking. Once you've drawn your dart outline or cut it out, pinch either side of the triangle with the fabric right sides together, and pin. Sew the sides together with a normal seam allowance.

That is honestly all there is to it! See how, all of a sudden, what would have been a flat pouch has some shape?

PATTERN

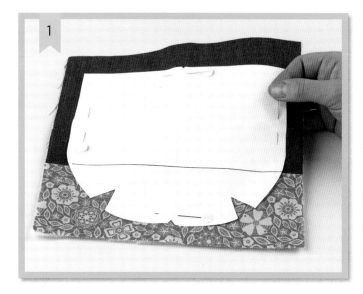

1 Begin by cutting two 15 x 28cm (6 x 11in) main pouch outer pieces from the denim and two 9 x 28cm (3½ x 11in) bottom pouch pieces from the contrasting fabric. Sew one denim outer to the contrasting fabric outer along one long edge, right sides together; repeat with the other two pieces. Fuse a piece of H630 to the back of each and trim to size. Place the template on top of one pair and line up the dividing line with the fabric join. Cut out the overall pouch shape, including the base darts. Repeat with the other pair. One will be the front piece, the other the back.

2 Use the template to cut out two lining pieces.

3 From the gold iron-on foils cut out the hashtag, 'selfie!!!' and an instant-photograph shape. Fuse them to the front outer panel, following the manufacturer's instructions.

TIP

Mix the foils you use for your alphabet embellishment. It looks particularly dramatic to use the gold glitter foil for the word 'selfie!!!' and the instant-photograph shape here, and then use regular gold foil for the hashtag. Have a play!

4 Prepare the zip: mark and tack/baste a line in from either end of the zip by 1.5cm (⅝in). Trim off the extra. Take your straight binding and cut it in half, so that you have a piece for each end of the zip. Fold one piece in half lengthways, tucking the folded raw edges inside. Glue the inside then encase one zip tape end. Repeat with the other zip tape end. Leave the binding to dry – clipping foldback/bulldog clips onto them will help keep them in place while they dry. Once dry, trim off the excess.

GATHER THESE SUPPLIES:

◉ Fabric
  - FQ of denim-style quilting cotton, for the main pouch outer
  - F8th of contrasting quilting cotton, for the bottom pouch outer
  - FQ of coordinating quilting cotton, for the lining
◉ Interfacing
  - Two 26 x 30cm (10½ x 12in) pieces of light-weight, non-woven, fusible wadding/batting: I have used H630 by Vlieseline®
◉ 18cm (7in) metal zip: I have used a denim effect zip
◉ 10cm (4in) length of 6cm (2⅜in) wide straight binding: mine has a denim effect, but you could use a scrap from the FQ denim fabric too – just make sure it is cut on the straight grain!
◉ Iron-on glittered gold foil: I have also used a scrap of plain gold foil to accent my hashtag, but that is optional
◉ Split ring, swivel clip and bead, to decorate the zipper pull
◉ Extra strong, all-purpose crafting glue (make sure it is clear drying)
◉ Your essential sewing kit (see page 11), plus zip foot
◉ Optional: A3 (11¾ x 16½in) piece of paper plus pencil to cut out alphabet and accent templates, manual die-cutting machine plus alphabet dies and instant-photograph-shaped die

TEMPLATE ON PATTERN SHEET A

WHAT WIDTH BINDING DOES MY BOUND-END ZIP NEED?

The binding can be any width at all actually, and it is a great way to make a zip a bit longer. Here is the maths: whatever length you trim the zip ends to, your binding must be four times that width. Mine are 1.5cm (⅝in) and four times that is 6cm (2½in).

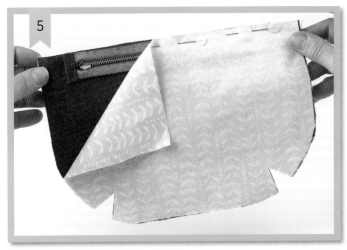

5 Let's make a zip sandwich! With the right side of one of your outer panels facing up, lay your bound zip on top, zip facing down and one long tape edge matching the top raw edge of the outer panel. Pin the lining over the top, right side facing down. Set up the zip foot on your sewing machine and sew across the top edge. Repeat on the other side of the zip tape with the remaining outer panel and lining piece.

6 Pinch your dart outlines together on both outer panel pieces and pin in place. Repeat with the lining pieces. Sew each dart together then press to one side – this stops the dart fabric from sticking up and creating bulk in the fabric.

> **TIP**
>
> When I sew darts, I like to shorten my stitch length and reverse stitch at the start to prevent the seam ends unravelling with use.

7 Pull the zip open if it's not already. Pin outer to outer and lining to lining. Then, leaving a 7.5cm (3in) gap in the bottom of the lining, sew around the perimeter of the pouch, over the darts too.

8 Turn the whole bag out through the gap. Close the gap in the lining with your machine, then stuff the lining back inside the pouch.

> **TIP**
>
> Once you turn out your pouch, see how nicely the end binding sits nicely with none of the puckering that you get with normal zip installation? If it is a bit squeezed, simply unpick that little section with a quick unpick then re-sew that section with a slightly smaller seam allowance.

9 Finish off your pouch with your zipper pull decoration! I fastened a pretty bead to a split ring, then attached this to the swivel clip. The clip then slid easily onto the zip pull.

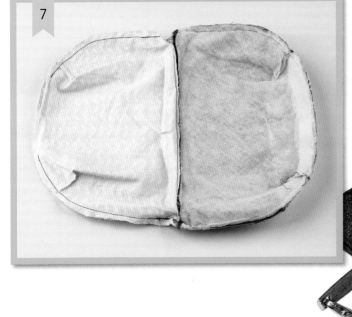

PUTTING IT ALL TOGETHER

Well, peeps; this is it!

Our sewing journey together is almost at an end and I do hope that you have enjoyed it and learned a lot of new skills. It is useful in these cases to look back to the beginning, as you can really appreciate the sheer amount of sewing distance that you have covered.

I have one last make for you now that not only features a number of techniques you should be a dab hand at doing, but that adds one more useful skill to your machine-sewing repertoire (because you're not getting away that easily...). Our last make is a super handy lined bag, with **patch/slip pockets** incorporated in the lining. Sounds scary, but really (especially after everything you've conquered already), this is not difficult at all.

WHAT YOU WILL LEARN:

- Finishing off your work neatly
- Making lined patch/slip pockets
- Preventing pocket sagging
- A slightly different pattern format

SEWING 101

Finishing off your work neatly

Before we get down to the project, and now that you're a more experienced sewist, I want to talk to you a little bit about finishing off your work. It is actually my pet hate to have ugly seams visible in bags and stuff badly tucked behind things in the hope no one will be looking! As a child, my mother showed a lot of arts and crafts in our district shows in Australia and she became the unbeaten floral art champion in the wider area. How? Strict attention to detail. She told me that judges would go looking for slip-ups in the made items, especially if they struggled to pick the winner. Things like: 'Is the back looking good?' 'Is there a mark or a loose bit?' These would be enough to tip the balance between the championship ribbon (or trophy), or nothing. Since then, I've grown up looking at details and finding ways to make things neat. I went on to steward and judge too, so the skills did not go to waste!

While you may not want to put your own sewing in a show, often poor attention to detail can sink your otherwise beautiful make when someone else looks at it. It can look homemade, not handmade, which is a pity. Neatness is not impossible, it requires just a little more attention to detail. Are your top threads matching the main fabric, and bobbin threads matching the lining fabric? Are there loose threads that need trimming off? In addition, our sewing machines and sewing methods are so sophisticated nowadays that it's not hard to achieve neatness!

This is where lining comes in. As you will have seen through several projects already, lining not only creates a lovely neat interior for your items, it is also a cunning way of hiding scrappy bits on the underside or inside of your work. For this reason, we're making a tote bag that features lining for a professional, scraggle-free finish!

Making lined patch/slip pockets

To add to the professional finish of our lined tote, we're going to make some nice, functional, lined pockets. Most pockets are one piece of fabric with a seam allowance sewn in place, which is then stitched onto the outside or inside of an item – have a look at any man's business shirt and you will see a patch/slip pocket. However, because this sort of pocket is made of one piece of fabric, it is not ideal for something like a bag as it is a bit flimsy. To make our bag pockets stronger and more functional, we're going to line them.

To make a lined patch/slip pocket, you need three pieces of fabric – one for the outer side of the pocket, one for the inside, and a piece of thin, fusible interfacing to pop in between the two. If the pocket is inside the bag, attached to the lining, the outer and inside of the pocket are usually the same. If the pocket is sitting on the front of the bag, there may be a feature fabric used inside the pocket for added fanciness. As luck would have it for teaching purposes, we have one of each kind of pocket! And both types of pockets are made in the same way.

So what do I mean by 'thin' interfacing? You need a soft, flexible, light-weight fusible interlining that will give the pocket gentle structure without any bulk, such as S320 by Vlieseline®.

To keep your pocket nice and slim, and reduce as much bulk as possible in the seams, we'll cut the S320 to the size of the pocket, then cut the outer and inside fabrics to about 2cm (¾in) larger all around. Once the interlining is fused centrally to one fabric piece, we'll sew the fused and non-fused pocket pieces right sides together. Your best sewing will be needed here, as the stitching must be straight, accurate and right on the edge of the interfacing, so that when the pocket is turned out the right way it will be perfect. Have no fear – you've been practising for this moment!

Preventing pocket sagging

Large pockets, such as the ones we'll be adding to our bag, can sag. There are two things that you can do about this. Either put some sort of closure on the pocket and base fabric, such as a snap fastener or button, or segment the pocket into smaller compartments using vertical top-stitching. Again, I'll be giving you a chance to learn both techniques! Personally, I quite like the second option because there is no bulk and it allows you to tailor your pocket compartments to a particular size, so you can put specific items in the pocket and have them stay put. Think about what you want to put into the pockets (like your mobile phone, pens, make-up) and go from there.

A slightly different pattern format

Before we get to the pattern (you know me by now; there is always one more thing), you will notice that the pattern this time has a slightly different format. This is a format you will no doubt encounter again in your sewing journey. There is a separate section for cutting, another for preparation and another for the main sewing. The reason for a 'cutting out' section is that, when you cut everything in one go, you can work out the best possible usage for your fabric and prevent wastage. The 'preparation' section allows you to prep ahead small components so that, when it comes to the sewing part of the pattern where you need them, the components are ready to go – this greatly helps the flow of the make. Things like handles, labels, tabs and sometimes zip prep will fall into this category.

The 'cutting out' section is popular so you will see it a lot, especially in quilting and patchwork patterns: as you need so many little pieces, all taken from a certain amount of fabric, it's much easier to have them cut out earlier on. The 'preparation' section is not as common, but it is useful to know what to do if you do encounter it.

PATTERN

That's it! The only thing left to do now is to make the bag itself. You have the skills! Remember, unless stated otherwise, all the seam allowances are 5mm (¼in) and your fabric is cut on the straight grain.

TO CUT

From the 90 x 60cm (35½ x 23¾in) piece of canvas:
- Two 45 x 40cm (17¾ x 15¾in) pieces, for the bag outer
- Two 66 x 4cm (26 x 1½in) strips, for the handle trims

From the 90 x 75cm (35½ x 30in) piece of coordinating cotton fabric:
- Two 45 x 40cm (17¾ x 15¾in) pieces, for the lining panels
- Four 21 x 15cm (8¼ x 6in) pieces, for the internal pockets
- 21 x 20cm (8¼ x 8in) piece, for the external front pocket lining

From the cotton webbing:
- Two straps, each 60cm (23½in) long

From the interfacing:
- 19 x 18cm (7½ x 7in) piece, for the external front pocket outer
- Two 19 x 13cm (7½ x 5in) pieces, for the internal pocket

PREPARATION

1 Fold over each long side of the canvas handle trim strips to the wrong side by 5mm (¼in) and press. Stick double-sided sticky tape down the centres of both webbing pieces and lay a pressed trim centrally onto each webbing strap. You'll notice the trims overhang at each end – this is correct! Fold these extra bits over the ends of the webbing and stick them in place too. Sew down each long side of the trims to secure. Treat the ends of the webbing with fray stopper.

> ## TIP
>
> Folding the trim ends under the end of the webbing looks neater and helps stop the majority of the webbing ends from fraying. It will be lovely and secure when you sew it on.

2 Fuse each piece of interfacing centrally to the wrong side of its corresponding pocket piece – the external front pocket outer and two of the internal pocket pieces from the coordinating cotton fabric.

3 Transfer the template on Pattern Sheet A onto your five chosen scrap pieces of fabric. Cut these out, then glue these appliqué shapes onto the right side of the needlecord piece.

> ## TIP
>
> It is helpful to draw a squarish border onto the front pocket outer first, using the edge of the interfacing (you will be able to just feel it on the front side), to help you work out where the motif should go: it should be centred nicely within the border.

GATHER THESE SUPPLIES:

- Fabric
  - 90 x 60cm (35½ x 23¾in) piece of canvas fabric, for the bag outer
  - 90 x 75cm (35½ x 30in) piece of coordinating cotton fabric, for the bag lining
  - 21 x 20cm (8¼ x 8in) piece of solid needle cord, for the bag front pocket
  - Five scraps of different-coloured solids, for making the heart-and-flower motif
- Interfacing
  - FQ of soft, flexible, light-weight fusible interlining: I have used S320 fusible interlining by Vlieseline®
- 1.2m (1⅓ yd) of 4cm (1½in) wide navy blue cotton webbing, for the handles
- Two gold snap fasteners plus snap pliers: I have used KAM snaps in size 20
- Extra-strong, all-purpose crafting glue (make sure it is clear drying)
- Fray stopper
- Double-sided sticky tape
- Your essential sewing kit (see page 11), plus darning foot

TEMPLATE ON PATTERN SHEET A

2

See how close I'm sewing to the interfacing here?

SEWING

4 Set up your sewing machine for FME, then embroider around the edges of the appliqué shapes. Go over the larger motifs at least twice, and don't worry about being too neat! As you sew around the leaves, remember to sew in the central vein, from the base of the leaf–partway along. When finished, trim all of the threads away.

5 Take one of the interfaced and un-interfaced internal pocket pieces then place them right sides together and pin. Here's the neat sewing bit! Set up your machine with the regular presser foot and, with the interfacing side facing up, sew right around the interfacing on the very edge, leaving a turning gap in the middle of one side.

6 Trim the seam allowance back to 5mm (¼in). When this is done, clip across the corners to reduce bulk.

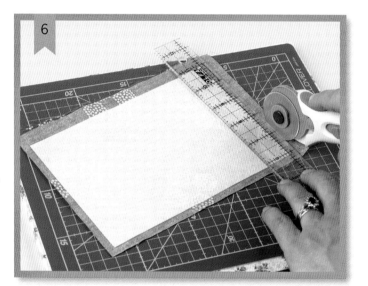

7 Now turn the pocket the right way out and press so that the edges are perfect. Repeat to make the other internal pocket, and the external front pocket. Don't sew the openings closed – we will do this later.

8 Top-stitch the external front pocket to the right side of one bag outer along the sides and bottom, closing the turning gap at the same time. The pocket should sit centrally 13cm (5in) down from one short edge (this will be the top of the bag). To help centre the pocket, fold it in half and finger press the fold to crease it slightly, and repeat with the bag outer. Line up the folds – perfectly in the middle! Attach a snap fastener to the top of the pocket to keep it secure and prevent sagging. (For guidance on placement, refer to the finished picture on page 121.)

> ## TIP
>
> Because of the motif, sectioning the outside pocket with vertical seams is not possible. A snap closure helps the pocket hold its shape instead.

Once you've turned the pocket through the gap and pressed it, you'll see that sewing close to the interfacing has allowed the stitching to sit along the very edge of the pocket. Very professional and neat, right?

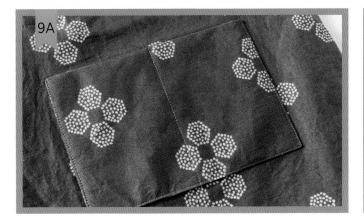

9A

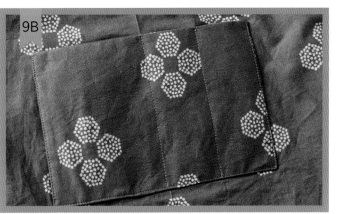

9B

9 Stitching as close to the edge as you can, top-stitch one internal pocket to the right side of one lining panel, closing the turning gap at the same time. The pocket should sit centrally, 10cm (4in) down from one short edge of the lining panel (this will be the top of the bag). Repeat with the other internal pocket piece with the remaining lining panel. When the pockets are in place, draw vertical lines down each one to section the pockets into smaller compartments. Top-stitch over these lines. A central divider [**A**] is useful, or you could add a couple of pen pockets [**B**].

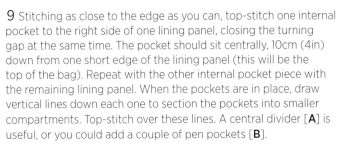

10 Sew the front and back bag outers right sides together, along the sides and bottom edge. Turn right side out. Do the same with the lining but, this time, leave a 7.5cm (3in) wide gap in the bottom seam. Keep the lining inside out.

11 To line the bag, pull the lining on over the outer so that the right sides are together. Match the top raw edges of both bag panels and their side seams, too, then pin. Sew around the top edge, leaving no gaps. Turn the bag out through the gap in the lining and close the gap by machine. Stuff the lining down into the bag and press the top edge so that it is perfect, then top-stitch all the way around it to keep the lining down. There – you have only just gone and lined a bag!

12 Attach the handles next. On the bag front, measure down 5cm (2in) from the top and 7.5cm (3in) from the side edges. Take one trimmed handle and, making sure the strap isn't twisted, attach each end to either side of the bag front by top-stitching a square over the ends. Repeat with the other handle on the back of the bag, ensuring it aligns with the front.

13 With the remaining snap fastener, attach the male half to the bag front and the female half to the lining against the bag back, both placed centrally along the top edges.

BOX BASING THE BAG

There is the option of boxing the base for your tote, as you did for the pot-plant cover (see page 46). It will increase the volume of your bag a bit by giving it a wider base, but it will take away some of the height. Before sewing your bag pieces together, cut 3cm (1¼in) squares from each bottom corner of the bag outer and lining, then sew the main sides and bottom edges of the bag panels only. Pinch the bottom and side seams together at each corner then sew across.

12

Finished! And, unfortunately, so is your sewing course. But this means that you can now machine sew, and all it takes from here on in is further practice and exploring new techniques.

This book is by no means a comprehensive list of everything-it-takes-to-be-a-sewist, but it does mean that you can make a lot of things and technically, you are no longer a beginner. Enjoy the world of sewing, spread those wings and keep on making!

INDEX

ACKNOWLEDGEMENTS

As usual, a book like this takes more than just the work of the person named on the front cover. I am indebted to the lovely team at Search Press for all of your tireless work (most of which I never know about) so to all, thank you! A special thank you to Katie French, for making it happen in the first place and thinking of me to do the job, and to Emily Adam, my editor extraordinaire, who has knitted all of my mad ramblings together into the product that you have now. A thank you also to Paul and Stacy, the most brilliant photographers. Honestly, I am constantly gobsmacked by the talent and ability of you both.

Of course, there are also the products that have gone into the projects. I am forever grateful to Pat and Walter Bravo from Art Gallery Fabrics for the most beautiful fabrics in the world, and to Paul and Jacqui Smith from Hantex for making the fabric appear so smoothly using your special magic. You can do no wrong.

Sharron at Vlieseline® deserves a special mention for the interfacings, and the amount of times that I have sent her, scissors in hand, to the warehouse. Thank you Sharron; my designs look the way they do because of your help.

Tonic Studios gave me some game-changing scissors and Berisfords have, to my mind, the finest ribbons anywhere in the universe. Thank you both!

And Clover! Thank you for some of the most amazing tools! I didn't know that I needed some of these things, and now I cannot imagine my life without them.

A big thank you to Sizzix®. I have been using your lovely and innovative products for a few years now, and it made me happy to use them here in my book where I could show my readers why I love them so much. Thank you Rebecca Jones for your support and for finding things for me to fit the bill exactly.

Finally, a huge thank you to Janome is called for, of course, since without them and their wonderful sewing machines, a book about machine sewing would just not happen. I use their Memory Craft 8200 QCP Special Edition every day for all of my sewing. To say that I would be lost without it would be the world's biggest understatement.

Of course, no acknowledgement would be complete without thanking the people closest to me – my family. A small group but perfectly formed, I could not possibly function without you. My husband, Rob, is the best chauffeur in the world; our son, Tristan, gives me a reason to shine; and my mum, Shirley, keeps up the never-ending stream of support and motherly pride. Daisy, my little cocker spaniel, provides the bossiness and snuggles – although I might say that her timing is sometimes a little off. Basically, my deadlines are not her problem!

Thank you, everyone – we have done it again!

Debbie xx